Planing *enjoyable* Reunions

Planing *enjoyable* Reunions

ALMA HEATON

This book is not an official publication of The Church of Jesus Christ of Latter-day Saints.

ISBN: 1-55517-376-4

10 9 8 7 6 5 4 3 2 1

Published and Distributed by:

925 North Main, Springville, UT 84663 • 801/489-4084

CFI Publishing and Distribution Since 1986

Cedar Fort, Incorporated

CFI Distribution • CFI Books • Council Press • Bonneville Books

Cover Design and Page Layout by Corinne A. Bischoff

Printed in the United States of America

Table of Contents

Preface

This book has been prepared and published because of the many requests for help in organizing family reunions.

In this book are suggestions for those who are anticipating their first reunion and helps, suggestions, and changes for those who have held reunions all their lives. This material is written in a systematic and logical manner.

Encouragement to publish this book also came from my family recreation class at BYU.

I was hooked on reunions at age sixteen when the Coxes spent a week in Flat Canyon in a camp-out reunion. We held rodeos every day. We went hiking and sliding down glaciers. We held talent shows at night, as well as danced to our own family orchestra. Since attending this reunion, I have regularly attended reunions on both sides of the family.

The suggestions in this book may also be used for class reunions, missionary reunions, reunions of near army buddies, etc.

Acknowledgments

For many years I have been gathering information from families that hold family reunions. Reading over their reunion outlines and programs has given me a broader view of the purpose of family reunions. I want to thank all the families that have helped in this way.

The following acknowledgment is not intended to relieve the author of his full responsibility, and I want to acknowledge the invaluable assistance rendered by my wife, Marie, and Mary Louise Seamons in editing the manuscript. Following through with details is acknowledged with the deepest feeling of gratitude.

Appreciation is also expressed to Mary Louise for typing the manuscript.

Last, but not least, I want to give credit to my father, uncles, aunts, and grandparents for instilling in me the desire to mingle with my family in family reunions.

Special thanks to Dian Thomas for giving permission to use some of her recipes from her book *Today's Tips for Easy Living*.

Thank you, Janie Thompson, for your stirring genealogy song.

Foreword

If you really want to know a relative to the extent of loving him, have fun with him. The more you know him, the more likely you will want to be around him and accept him.

Reunions are very important when you consider that everyone has a chance to tie himself to a family in a patriarchal order. The family reunion is the place to give of yourself, love others, and develop the feeling of belonging.

A successful reunion will compensate for all the time, work, and money that it has taken to organize and prepare it.

A commitment for an assignment given to a family member may be just the thing for uninterested family members. Of course, the best way to keep a family interested is to have fun. Happiness is everyone's goal.

Some families have reunions just for older folks and others for the younger folks. The Heaton family finds all ages together makes for a better reunion.

Our immediate family has a family reunion every year. Grandfather's family has a reunion every five years. Some people have reunions twice a year. Some families get together at every holiday, others for deer hunting season, etc. Reunions should be a tradition for all family members.

Family History

Four score and seven years ago our forefathers brought forth on this continent a new family, conceived and dedicated to the proposition that all men should eventually leave their mothers and fathers and cleave unto a wife and multiply and replenish the earth.

We are now met in a great reunion of that ancestral line to share that family life with other families so conceived and dedicated to the same eternal purposes, and we are determined, convinced, and committed to the proposition that this family will not perish from the earth.

Finding Lost Relatives

We often hear of the happiness one receives when finding a dead relative, but have you heard of the joy that comes to a family when a living relative is found?

I want to relate one experience that could have happened only at a family reunion.

We were all camped at a family reunion in a beautiful canyon when here came a string of cars. The strangers drove up and asked if this was a Cox reunion. We said it was. "Well, put 'er there," and we shook hands. "We are your long-lost cousins."

After convincing us they were telling the truth, we had double the tents spread out over the canyon floor.That night during the family program they told us this story.

During the Gold Rush in California, a couple became sick and were nursed back to health by the Mormons. Yes, they were converted. Since being converted, they wanted a family, but they could not have a family of their own because a doctor had fixed them up at their request, so they could not have children.

When Bro. Richardson went to President Brigham Young for advice, President Young told Bro. Richardson to divorce his wife. President Young told Sis. Richardson he would pick three of the best men in the church; then she could pick one of the three to father her children. Brother Richardson said that was the hardest thing he ever did — to divorce his wife.

Sister Richardson chose Walter Cox, my real uncle, for a husband, and they were married. After the third child was born, they got a divorce, and Bro. and Sis. Richardson were married again and moved to Arizona with the three children.

This was kept a secret for many years. Then the truth came out, and the descendants of Mr. and Mrs. Richardson wanted to meet the relatives on the Cox side of the family. Those three children had a lot of descendants. This great posterity was the group that unexpectedly chose a family reunion in which to tell their story. They have attended many Cox reunions since that eventful day.

Overview

In 1984, all families in the Church were given two assignments in priesthood family history:

1. To establish a family organization
2. To keep meaningful and accurate family records

These assignments, which pertain to our living family members and our descendants, provide a beginning place for those who have not been engaged in family history research. They are also very fundamental responsibilities regardless of precious activity and background in family histories.

These assignments should be prayerfully considered by all family heads. Priesthood leaders and home teachers are available to counsel with the family regarding appropriate goals and means for accomplishing them.

President Harold B. Lee said, "When the full measure of Elijah's mission is understood...it applies just as much on this side of the veil as it does to the other side of the veil. So, the hearts of you fathers and mothers must be turned to your children right now, if you have the true spirit of Elijah.

Family Organization and Records

Behold, the time has fully come, which was spoken of by the mouth of Malachi — testifying that he [Elijah] should be sent, before the great and dreadful day of the Lord come —

To turn the hearts of the fathers to the children, and the children to the fathers, lest the whole earth be smitten with a curse —

Therefore, the keys of this dispensation are committed into your hands; and by this ye may know that the great and dreadful day of the Lord is near, even at the doors.

D&C 110:14-16

1984 Objectives for Every Family

Family Organization Assignment

Implement the principles of family organization on the three levels shown below, beginning with the immediate family and adapting to family needs and circumstances.

Three Levels of Organization

1. The immediate family organization should be involved in the following:
    a. Missionary work
    b. Family preparedness (welfare)
    c. Family history and temple work
    d. Other family needs (such as teaching the gospel, cultural and social activities, etc.)

2. The grandparent family should be organized for the same purposes as the immediate family.
3. The ancestral family should be organized for coordinating family history activity on common ancestral lines.

Family Records Assignment

1. Set in order personal and family histories and recorded testimonies and counsel and bring them up-to-date.
2. Review your family history records, (including the four-generation program, to discover possible errors and poor documentation. These records must be accurate to be "worthy of all acceptation."

Content of Family Records

Family records might contain a variety of information concerning these topics:

1. Loved ones and friends
2. Ordinances received.
3. Spiritual impressions and testimonies
4. Answers to prayers
5. Adversities and failures
6. Blessings and triumphs
7. Travels
8. Important dates and places
9. Lessons learned
10. Photographs
11. Priesthood blessings (such as father's blessings, patriarchal blessings, etc.)
12. Priesthood lineage

13. Pedigrees and family group records
14. Minutes of family meetings, councils, and interviews
15. Family goals and assignments
16. Church callings

In the October 1974 General Conference, President Spencer W. Kimball asked members of the Church to get to know their relatives; there is no better way than through family reunions.

Family reunions have always played an important part in social and religious life. Even before our Father in Heaven sent us to earth, He called His sons and daughters together in the Spirit World for a great and important reunion. At that time the pattern and purposes of reunions were set.

We had the opportunity to get acquainted, receive instructions for God's purposes, and make decisions as to our future, choosing our leader and making commitments to follow Him. We decided at that time we wanted our free agency and to organize for the success of the family program outlined during this great family reunion.

Adam, Enoch, Noah, Abraham, Isaac, and Jacob followed this pattern. When they came to these reunions and followed instructions, they were successful. Those that did not come to Noah's reunion were washed away. Many others followed this same pattern. Joseph called his family to reunite in Egypt. Lehi called his family to reunite in a new world, just as we may do if we follow the Lord's instructions.

In this day the Lord has revealed through His servants, the prophets, that the most important unit on earth is the family unit, and the way for the family to be successful in every phase of life is to regularly meet together and follow the reunion plans. When we disobey this commandment, we suffer as did the family of Judah.

I am grateful to my great-grandfather who was called by Brigham Young to gather his family together in southern Utah. As far back as I can remember, the Heaton family has regularly held reunions.

The Family is the Unit of Exaltation

The family is the most important organization to which a person will ever belong. The celestial kingdom is based on the family relationship.

> In the highest heaven or degree of the Celestial Kingdom individuals are organized into families. Each family group will consist of perfected parents and perfected children. They will maintain this relationship eternally. Yet each family will be a unit in a veritable chain of families (A.F. Bennett, *Searching with Success*, Deseret Book Company, Salt Lake City, Utah, 1962, p. 249).

> A family organization can unite living individuals in purpose and ideal. It can foster mutual love and understanding that comes from working together towards a common goal and can thus prepare them while yet in mortality for eventual eternal unity (*Ten Basic Steps in Genealogy*, Genealogical Society, Salt Lake City, Utah, 1963, p. 15).

Members of the family are given a chance to get to know one another by working together in a common purpose. If you really know a person, you will love him.

> The idea of a family organization is to get the family together to work toward a family goal. The preservation of a family heritage, family traditions, family history and a family genealogy are reasons enough for effecting a family organization. When this is coupled with family fellowship and the strengthening of family ties through love and mutual understanding, the situation becomes ideal (Priesthood Correlation in Family History Program, p. 39).

Each family has those who like to do family history research or temple work, those who like to write family history or attend reunions, or those who seem to be content in providing finances for these projects. A family organization is designed to bring them all together and, while not dimming each individual's 'first great love' in the least, gives all a chance to participate in the entire program. And won't it be glorious to find each member of such a great family having earned his place in the Celestial kingdom?

Elder Theodore M. Burton

Family Organization

It is important for us...to cultivate in our own family a sense that we belong together eternally.... We ought to encourage our children to know their relatives. We need to talk of them, make an effort to correspond with them, visit them, join family organizations, etc.

President Spencer W. Kimball

It seems to me there is nothing more important for a priesthood leader or a priesthood holder to do than to give consideration to the fact that he is establishing his patriarchal order here in mortal life, and that that order will be extended into the eternities.

President Ezra Taft Benson

Get a notebook...a journal that will last through all time, and maybe the angels may quote from it for eternity. Begin today and write in it your goings and comings, your deepest thoughts, your achievements and your failures, your associations and your triumphs, your impressions and your testimonies. Remember, the Savior chastised those who failed to record important events.

Spencer W. Kimball

In every family a record should be kept of the immediate family. It should be a book known and used in the family circle; and when the child reaches maturity and goes out to make another household, one of the first things that the young couple should take along should be the records of their families, to be extended by them as life goes on.

Elder John A. Widtsoe

Why Organize?

It provides goals. You're going someplace. It makes you a doing *family. Organizing saves time, fixes responsibility, and puts each one to work without duplication and wasted effort. It makes it possible to pool many resources. It is a standard bearer. It is a visible symbol of pride in one's origin and destiny. Organization helps you recall memories going by and to look forward to those that are coming. A family letter cannot be circulated unless we have some semblance of organization. Family records cannot be gathered without committees and assignment.*

Dr. Harold Glen Clark

Organization Meeting Checklist

I. Getting the family together. If you are just getting started on a family reunion do the following:

A. Start an address file

1. Aunts
2. Uncles
3. Cousins
4. More distant relatives

B. Go visiting to as many relatives as possible

1. Tell them of intent and scope
2. Begin making plans
3. Ask for names and addresses of others

C. Write letters

1. To all those you can't visit
2. Ask for names and addresses of others

D. Arrange a meeting

   1. Advertise so all can attend
   2. Elect officers
   3. Organize officially
   4. If a meeting cannot be arranged, the organization can be handled by correspondence.

II. Types of Family Organizations

A. The immigrant ancestor

   1. His ancestors
   2. His descendants

B. The patriotic ancestor organization (or prominent ancestor)

C. The early LDS convert

D. A single family organization (only two generations — your family)

E. The multi-generation (three or four)

F. The surname (a particular surname with all its spelling variations)

G. The reunion organization (officers and committee elected each year to plan the next family reunion)

III. Officers

A. President

   1. Overall management
   2. Coordinator

B. Vice-President (or vice-presidents)

   1. To assist the president
   2. One in charge of each separate division of the organization — either a locality or a family line

C. Secretary

   1. Official correspondence
   2. Maintains records

D. Treasurer

   1. Knowledge of finance
   2. Bookkeeping

E. Genealogist

1. To organize research
2. To analyze results of searches

F. Historian

1. Someone with writing talent to write individual or family histories.

G. Reunion Director (appointed by the president each year)

IV. Large Family Organization

A. Board of Governors (or Directors)
B. Social Committee
C. Reunion Committee
D. Finance Committee
E. Membership Committee
F. Publication Committee

V. Constitution and By-laws

A. Article I (Name of organization)
B. Article II (Objective)
C. Article III (Membership)
D. Article IV (Meetings)
E. Article V (Officers)
F. Article VI (Committees)
G. Article VII (Amendments)
H. By-laws
    1. Section 1 (Duty of Executive Committee)
    2. Section 2 (Duty of President)
    3. Section 3 (Duty of Vice-President)
    4. Section 4 (Duty of Secretary)
    5. Section 5 (Duty of Treasurer)
    6. Section 6 (Duty of Genealogist)
    7. Section 7 (Duty of Historian)
    8. Section 8 (Dues)
    9. Section 9 (Amendments)

VI. Filing System
   A. Name and address
   B. Correspondence files
   C. Research file
   D. Family Group Records file
   E. Family Index file
      1. Each family group
      2. Each individual name

VII. Family Representative (for submitting records to Genealogical Society)
   A. May be the genealogist
   B. Must be a living blood relative

The Purpose of Family Reunions

A family reunion can be a very personal and privileged gathering — jumping with fun, laughter, and reminiscences. It's a time for the "grands" and the "great-grands" to inspect and enjoy the newer additions, a time for all ages to exchange notes on the past year. If you have never organized a reunion — or even if you're a veteran at it — you'll find ideas here on how to do it up just right.

Family reunions are really an extension of family home evenings. That is, they are an opportunity to usher our larger, eternal families together to work at common problems, learn to understand and love one another, and unite ourselves in the work of the Lord just as we do in family home evenings.

Perhaps another real purpose of family reunions is to have positive, enjoyable experiences together to cement family relationships. Having fun together is a powerful and effective way to bring a family together. The lasting memories that are formed in well-planned family reunions will add to the respect and love that we hope to have for each other throughout eternity.

Family reunions also provide real opportunity for the younger members of the family to become acquainted with their heritage and relatives. Perhaps this heritage is part of the *sealing* force between the children and the fathers, to which Elijah referred. Through this heritage everyone has a chance to tie himself to a family in a patriarchal order.

Reunions are also an excellent way to organize and gather genealogical information and stimulate genealogical research. Often we spend a great deal of time researching our ancestors, and we fail to record the marriages, new babies, temple endowments, and other information of our own family. Certainly our living relatives are as important as our dead ones!

If family home evenings are some of the most important meetings conducted among Church members today, then family reunions must be just as important because family reunions are extensions of family home evenings.

The Reunion

Date

Selecting the wrong time of year for a family get-together can be disastrous. The best time is when the most members can attend. Perhaps one of the best times is when the family is already free for a state or national holiday. It is also a helpful idea to schedule the reunion at the same time each year. In this way, members of the family can plan a year ahead.

Place

Pick the reunion spot with care. Avoid crowded parks or lake areas. Make sure there are adequate sanitary facilities, such as running water, restrooms, and sufficient picnic tables and chairs. If, for instance, a park is chosen, reservations may need to be made months ahead of time.

The selection of a place for a family reunion will also be a key factor in the success of the family reunion. If the theme of the reunion calls for a lot of genealogical papers to be spread out and a lot of writing to be done by many people, being indoors under shelter from wind and rain is important. If there is a large banquet involving a lot of food and tables, a ward or stake cultural hall might be considered. For summertime reunions, look for a good grassy spot for the youth to play. A fenced-in area for toddlers, with plenty of play equipment, will require fewer adults to supervise them. An area large enough for volleyball, softball, and foot races should be considered, whether it is around a chapel or in a canyon. Trees are useful not only for shade but also for all types of swings and recreation equipment. If a temple session is on the program, the reunion should be held near a temple.

The location of the reunion can be the same each year if the family is not too scattered; otherwise, it would be well to rotate the location so that each member would have the opportunity of attending when the reunion is in his or her locality. If the family is large, then separate reunions may be held for each geographic area with a vice-president in charge of each, or each branch of the family may wish to meet separately with the director of that branch in charge.

Invitations

Making creative, original, and unique invitations may take a little thinking, but they are an absolute necessity if the reunion is to be a success. Often, a family will decide to attend simply on the strength of a creative invitation — a dull invitation may mislead them into thinking that the reunion will be dull. Besides announcing the theme, time, and place, an invitation should mention the program and the fun things that are going to happen. Ask for the number of people from the family who will attend. The reunion director (or chairman) should send announcements to everyone concerned, from newlyweds to older folks. A picture of last year's reunion could be included, as well as the up-to-date history of the family and newsletter. The invitation should also mention that each family should come prepared with some type of entertainment to take part in the program. Each family should also be reminded to bring genealogical information.

Send reunion songs with your invitations and give situations in which to sing them on the way to the reunion. Songs are found in this book under programs.

The Chairman of the reunion should be aware of the equipment needed for a successful and complete reunion. Whether the reunion is outdoors or indoors, there should be a source of electrical power. Lights, cameras, screens, microphones, loudspeakers, overhead projectors, film projectors, slide projectors, a record player, and a tape recorder should always be handy.

Planning

The executive committee should meet in advance of the reunion to formulate plans for the coming year and to make final arrangements for the reunion. If separate reunions are held, then it might be necessary for the supervising genealogist to meet with the family researcher at each reunion to coordinate the research program and to make research assignments.

A clan roundup may seem like a wonderful idea — and it can be — but there are hazards. You may have a wide span of age groups, as well as families who come from different environments and who are virtual strangers to each other. In your planning, strive to get everybody into the act by providing them with something to do, and see to it that they are all included in the activities and the preplanning.

The Big Day Dawns

Any minute now the family will start to arrive at the host home. The first duty is to get everyone settled. When a number of relatives live in close proximity, they should split housing chores for those staying for the weekend. Make sure no one's home bulges at the seams. The nearest hotel or motel might be the best answer. Manage the "setting in" for incoming relatives before you take off for the appointed reunion spot.

Special Touches

The chairman or committee should choose people to be responsible for food, location, MC of the program, and all special details.

Choose one relative's home as a gathering place before take-off for the reunion spot — particularly if it is in a canyon area. Families may come from a considerable distance and need an hour's rest before further driving. Plan on one "pack-horse" car or station wagon. This is one time you don't want to skimp on the equipment; everything from hammocks to play equipment and headache pills may come in handy.

A Few Special Touches for Special Occasions

Start a "chain gang" going to pack the supplies in the "pack-car" or small trailer. Don't forget all the other necessities you'll need besides food. Take along comforts for the very old and the very young. Beach umbrellas or pup tents might come in handy if there is no shade. You'll need a first-aid kit with remedies for bugs, scratches, and churning stomachs. (Count on it — someone will overeat.) Don't forget a good supply of games to suit all ages. Balloons and balls of all sizes are a must.

The "pack-car" with trailer should start out well in advance — with two of the strongest, most willing males driving. They can begin to set up the party scene before the rest of the family arrives. Space the departure of the cars ten minutes apart, using the "buddy system" again. A long cavalcade can slow up traffic and cause confusion.

Ways to Make a Reunion Run Smoothly

Distribute big name tags and pins. If desired, have everyone write down his name and the most important thing that's happened to him in the last year. This may seem obvious, but when a family is large, relationships grow very complex.

Plan to serve the meal no later than two hours after arrival. Say you arrive at 10:00 a.m. Serve substantial fare at noon and at four — before departing.

Be sure to bring cameras; also, someone could bring a motion picture camera. Everyone will want pictures as mementos. One member of the family is sure to have an instant-developing camera. This is the time for a team of camera buffs to go to work. Bring along a large bulletin board and set up the pictures just like a family tree, connecting the groupings with colored tape. Pin on small white cards with names and relationships. This is great fun, and any opportunistic youngster stands to make himself a tidy sum taking extra pictures on commission.

All family history equipment, including blank family group sheets, pedigree charts, old family pictures, family histories, and other genealogy forms, should be provided. Of course, tables are a must for eating, doing genealogy, and making displays of such items as books of remembrance and old family pictures.

Displays Are Impressive

I. Wall displays showing family lineal charts, bringing ancient ancestral records down to the living generation

II. Scriptural quotations, family sayings, etc.

III. Family picture displays and ideas developed by family members

IV. Book of remembrance displays from various families, open to browsing

V. Exchange tables, with a duplicating machine so families can exchange sheets and history information

VI. A four-generation responsibility corner to help those in need of help on this assignment and allow the ones who have technical knowledge to share it

VII. An antique table to show the family heirlooms and early tools, dishes, and handiwork

VIII. If a lecture method is used at all, it should include some family history, jokes, faith-promoting instances and *not* exceed 7 minutes

Organizational Meeting

One of the last items on the agenda is the organizational meeting in which to organize for the next reunion. The chairman again takes charge long enough to select a new reunion director, time, and place.

The new reunion director may want a few minutes to discuss ideas for the next reunion and to select new officers to help him. An up-to-date list of addresses, as well as old records, should be turned over to the new officers. A stirring family lecture and a commitment from the whole gang will help bring them back the following year. A discussion of reunion finances should also be included.

During this planning meeting, the youth could be engaged in activities rather than attending the organizational meeting. It is possible that a younger person could very well be on the entertainment or activity committee and should attend the meeting. If the youth have a voice in what projects are planned, they will support them more fully.

Planning for the Next Reunion
(or Choosing a Chairman for Next Year's Reunion)

Organizing the family is an essential step to successful reunions. A family organization is not complete until a person has been specifically chosen as chairman to direct and supervise reunions for the family. The family chairman directs the family organizational meeting and supervises the election of officers from year to year. Once a family member has been appointed chairman, he should determine where and when the family would like the reunion and then suggest an enthusiastic relative from the chosen locality to be the director of the reunion. The local director should be appointed yearly, as the site changes, but be approved by all those at the reunion. After the chairman and the director have been appointed, the director should choose a vice-chairman, secretary, and treasurer. It might be helpful if the secretary and treasurer are either from the director's family or live in the same locality.

MC Work

You are in charge of the entertainment for a family reunion. What do you do? Here you will find some helps that will make those attending interested. The most important responsibility of an MC is to make the program a success. Several things contribute to the fulfillment of the entertainment. If there are problems, an MC needs to take care of them before the program. He should be aware of what is going on at all times as well as have foresight into problems. Maybe it's finding a substitute for a number at the last minute or changing the program to have the best number last on the program.

The MC needs to plan for and arrange the various numbers in the most logical sequence. To do this, he needs to visit the various families before the program begins and find out how many in the family are participating. If the M.C. is prepared and enthusiastic, the program will not drag. The M.C. should prepare some humor to maintain attention and help get the crowd to respond and applaud after each number.

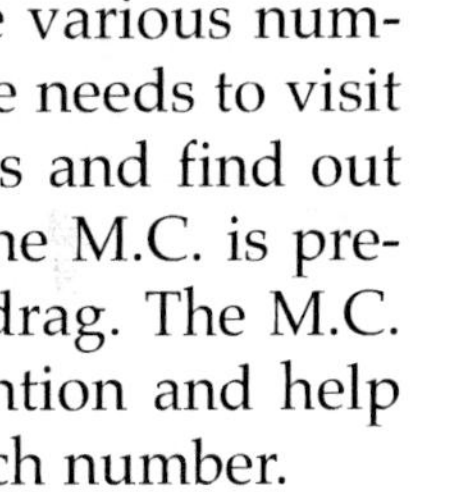

After the MC receives a list of entertainers and their presentations, he should arrange the numbers for the most pleasing effect. Sometimes a mediocre number can be better if the MC shows a lot of enthusiasm and introduces the participants correctly. Another quality an MC should possess is tact. A tactful MC can avoid embarrassing moments and hurt feelings. To know how much freedom to give a participant can be cause for concern, especially if there is a time limit. The more the MC knows

about each individual, the better he can evaluate all aspects of the program.

The types of programs are numerous. This is another reason for the MC to have a rich background of experience, if at all possible. With a small group, the MC can give more freedom than with a large group. When all are strangers, the problems might be to get the audience to react and become responsive. This may require the MC to be an entertainer himself. Discipline problems and off-color jokes should not be allowed.

Program

Families should not do the same thing year after year. A good program is important because it not only gives everyone a chance to get acquainted, but it can be as much fun as any part of the reunion. The program needs to have variety as well as excitement.

One of the most exciting parts of the program may be when grandpa and grandma tell stories of the older days, as well as sing the songs that were popular when they fell in love. It will be a spiritual feast to bear a newly returned missionary report. Some families select a different ancestor to honor each year. Even though some families may not come prepared to participate on the program, remembering them is still important; consequently, the M.C. should be prepared with some readings or skits that thoses families can do impromptu.

A FRIGHTFULLY GOOD DEAL!

Favorite songs of great-grandfather could be sung and century-old dances could be danced. For decorations, old farm machinery, scrubbing boards, and other old tools could be used. Games and activities that great-grandfather played could be used for the activity section of the program. For the program, old-timers could tell experiences of what it was like when they were young. There could also be a skit about a humorous event in the life of one of the ancestors.

One good way to identify individual families in the whole group is to have all wear hats, T-shirts, or some similar item.

These are things you can do to boost attendance and participation:

Prizes for various categories:	**Prize:**
Uncle that is best preserved	A jar of preserves
Family that came longest distance	Corn plasters
Family with most redheads	Pair of hand clippers
Family that weighs the most	Reducing pills
Family whose ages add up highest	Calendars
Best family identification	Badges

Honor the Elderly

Choose one of the oldest family members to honor. This can be funny or serious, poetic or plain. Tell of their accomplishments and contributions to the family. Show pictures of the elderly on an opaque projector.

This is Your Life

Choose a couple, family, or just one person and use the format of the TV show "This is Your Life." This can be effective, if well planned.

Traditional Anecdotes or Stories

The type of stories such as a special spiritual experience or a tale of crossing the plains needs to be passed on from generation to generation. These stories need to be told often. There are many creative ways to do this.

Films

Show a video of last year's reunion. Many different types can be shown, preferably those made at family reunions of those families attending. Films can be shown by family members depicting some ancestral experience. There is no end to creativity along this line.

Reader's Theatre

Important experiences of ancestors or family missionaries, etc., can be written up beautifully and read by family members with or without music in the background. This can be serious or funny, but should be accurate and informative.

Skits

Short, funny skits are very effective. They can be used to keep elders awake or to make the youngsters laugh.

Acknowledgment of Contest Winners

The committee members for the next family reunion could sponsor a contest. They pick a subject such as a family personality, history, town, or country important in genealogy, etc., and the entrants pick how they want to enter. Their enteries could be poetry, short stories, essays, or in musical form. The committee picks the winners, and they are presented during the reunion. This encourages members to use their talents and also to learn more about their heritage.

Another activity that can be fun is for families to memorize their genealogy. If your reunion is for all the descendants of your grandfather on your father's side, each person should be able to recite, when challenged, his name, his father's name, his mother's name, his grandfather's and grandmother's names. Whoever can do this receives a prize. If someone slips up, the one giving the challenge can take away his prize, which has not been opened. Cousins are sometimes surprised to find that their grandparents are also the grandparents of someone else.

Food

Everyone Has to Eat

If a meal is part of the agenda, just after or just before the program is a good time to eat. At this time, the people are together, and it is easier to explain to the entire gang what is to follow. The meal can add a great deal to the reunion. Some families have established a tradition of barbecuing a whole leg of beef or a small pig for large reunions. Other families plan a meal around the same fare that great-grandfather had. In this way, not only does the meal add to the theme, but it also provides an added incentive for all the relatives to be there.

There are several ways to approach the meal planning process.

1. Each family can take its own food and eat all together.
2. Each family can take its own food plus a salad to be cleared. All the salads are then sampled by other families.
3. Each family takes its own food, but the committee furnishes the drink and the dessert.
4. The committee assigns a menu so each family is eating the same food, and no one is envious of the food of the other families.
5. The committee assigns the menu so each family is responsible for one meal for everyone.
6. When the committee cooks the food for everyone, it makes more work for some, but enables the hosts to cook unusual things such as pig, a small calf, or lamb.

Chickens cooked in dutch ovens are delicious, and a variety of things can be cooked by this method in an open pit or by charcoal briquets. The cast is shared by the families.

7. If the reunion is just for one night and there are enough people involved, the meal can be catered.

Since most reunions take place during the summer and are outside, the picnic approach is generally used. Care should be taken to make sure the food you take along is safe to eat, whether you're planning a picnic in the park or an extended camping trip.

The best food choices include breads, hard cheeses, chilled hard-boiled eggs (left in the shell), canned meals and seafood, baked beans, packaged luncheon meats, clean fresh fruits and vegetables, and beverages such as juices. Chill perishables at home; then pack them in a well-insulated cooler with ice.

If you're taking a mayonnaise or oil-based salad for a side dish or sandwiches, pack the salad ingredients separately from the dressing in your cooler. Combine at serving time. Fried chicken, baked ham, and raw meats for grilling should be placed (lightly wrapped and well chilled) in the bottom of the cooler.

Custards, puddings, cream pies, and similar creamed foods should be kept at home, since they are susceptible to bacterial growth.

Use blue ice in your cooler — it holds up longer than ice cubes. Or fill plastic containers with water and freeze them for take-along refrigeration. Gallon plastic jugs such as those sold with milk are excellent. Also, plastic jugs filled with punch can be frozen and used as ice and then used as a beverage as they thaw. Water and milk can be used the same way. (Dairies claim freezing milk does not hurt the contents.) Don't use dry ice — it causes freezer burn if it touches the food or you. Heavy duty zippered plastic bags, filled three fourths full of water and frozen, can be placed covering the bottom of your ice chest. Not only does this save time and money, but there isn't any messy water in the bottom of your ice chest. These bags stay frozen a long time, and you don't waste water as you use it to rinse your hands, in cooking, or even to cool the car's radiator if it overheats and as the ice melts.

Remember that the main entertainment is enjoying each other's company as you prepare the meal together and dine together — so allow plenty of time for fun!

Bring along a portable barbecue so all ages can roast their own franks and pop their own popcorn. Prepare the ice cream at home and let it mellow in two or more ice cream makers while you're driving to the site. When it's dessert time, the honest-to-goodness homemade yumminess of the rich, velvety strawberry ice cream will draw raves from both the juniors and the seniors. Never mind if faces and fronts get a little messy. It'll all come out in the wash, except perhaps for Granddad's tie (and he has plenty of replacements to drag out).

Food, Food, and More Food

Meatloaf in an onion

An unusual family treat

1 lb. lean ground beef

1 egg

1/4 cup cracker crumbs

1/4 cup tomato sauce

1/8 teaspoon pepper

1/2 teaspoon salt

1/2 teaspoon dry mustard

6 large onions, peeled

Cut 6 12x14-inch rectangles of heavy-duty foil; set aside. In a medium bowl, mix ground beef, egg, cracker crumbs, tomato sauce, pepper, salt, and dry mustard. Set aside. Cut onions in half horizontally and remove centers, leaving 1/4-inch shell. Chop onion centers. Stir 1 tablespoons into meat mixture. Spoon meat mixture into 6 onion halves, rounding on top. Place remaining onion halves on top of filled onion halves. Place 1 filled onion on each piece of foil. Bring ends of foil up over onion. Fold foil down in small folds. Press sides of foil close to onion. Flatten ends and roll toward onion. Cook on coals 14 to 20 minutes on each side. Serves 6.

Peanut Butter and Honey Mix

When your peanut butter jar is half empty, add homogenized honey to taste and mix. It'll save time and mess when you want to make a quick peanut butter-and-honey sandwich. Use within one month.

From Dian Thomas, *Today Tips for Easy Living* (Tucson, Arizona: H.P. Book).

Upside-Down Cake in a Dutch Oven

A treat to cook and eat

1 (16 oz.) can pineapple slices

2 tablespoons butter or margarine

1 (8 oz.) jar maraschino cherries

1/2 cup packed brown sugar

1 (18 1/2 oz.) pkg. cake mix

Drain fruit, reserving pineapple juice. Line dutch oven with foil. Grease foil. Arrange pineapple with cherries in center of each slice on top of foil. Sprinkle brown sugar and 3 tablespoons of reserved juice over fruit. Prepare mix according to package directions. Pour over fruit. Put cover on dutch oven.

To bake, place in fireplace 1 inch above coals. Legs of oven should keep bottom of oven 1 inch above coals. If oven does not have legs, place on bricks. Use logs or shovel to arrange coals on top of the dutch oven. Bake 25 to 30 minutes or until a toothpick inserted in center of cake comes out clean. Cool 8 minutes in pan then invert onto platter. Carefully peel away foil.

Chili Dogs on a Bun

For a treat, try a hot dog with chili in a thermos. Tie a 12-inch length of dental floss around hot dog and heat in saucepan with chili. Lower hot dog into thermos with string hanging out the top. Pour chili around hot dog and cap thermos. Use end of floss to pull hot dog from chili into bun. Pull floss through dog and spoon chili onto bun for delicious chili dog.

Cake in Orange Cups

Bake your cake in the coals, too!

12 to 18 oranges

1 (18-1/2 oz.) pkg. yellow cake mix

Cut 12 to 18 12-inch squares of heavy-duty foil; set aside. Cut 1-inch slice from top of each orange. Scoop out orange fruit and pulp. Leave peel intact as a baking cup. Prepare cake according to package directions. Fill each orange peel 2/3 full with prepared cake batter. Replace top of each orange. Place one filled orange in center of foil piece. Bring foil together at top and twist to make airtight. Place in coals for 15 to 20 minutes. Serves 12 to 18.

Banana Boat

A delicious dessert to cook in coals

4 bananas, unpeeled

1/2 cup milk-chocolate pieces

1/2 cup miniature marshmallows

Cut a wedge-shaped section in each banana. Pull back peel. Remove wedge-shaped piece of banana. Fill cavity with milk-chocolate chips and marshmallows. Replace peeling over filling. Wrap securely in heavy-duty foil. Heat about 5 minutes over coals until chocolate and marshmallows melt. Serves 4.

Banana Dog

Spread peanut butter and honey on a hot dog bun. Wrap in plastic and place in lunch sack with banana. At lunchtime, peel banana and place in hot dog bun for an unusual treat.

Hot Chili Chips in a Bag

Take along individual corn-chip bag or put chips in self-sealing bag. Open bag and pour hot chili from thermos over chips. Bring along plastic spoon and enjoy chili chips in a bag. A great idea for football games on a cold day.

Tin-Can Ice Cream

Ice cream without an ice cream maker

1 cup milk
1 cup whipping cream
1/2 cup sugar
1/2 teaspoon vanilla extract
Nuts or fruit as desired
1 egg (optional)

Put all ingredients in a 1-pound coffee can with a tight-fitting plastic lid. Place lid on can. Place can with ingredients inside a #10 can. Pack remaining space in #10 can with salt and ice pieces. Roll back and forth on a table or cement slab for 10 minutes. Open outer can. Remove inner can with ingredients. Remove lid. Use a rubber spatula to stir up mixture; scrape sides of can. Replace lid. Drain ice water from larger can. Insert smaller can; pack with more ice and salt. Roll back and forth for five more minutes. Makes about 3 cups.

Fruit Pudding Refresher

For an extra treat, serve this salad in a flowerpot!

1 (20 oz.) can pineapple chunks in juice

2 bananas, sliced

1 cup shredded coconut

1 (11 oz.) can mandarin oranges, drained

1 (16 oz.) can fruit cocktail with juice

1 (3-3/4 oz.) pkg. instant lemon pudding mix

In medium bowl, combine pineapple chunks and juice with bananas, oranges fruit cocktail with juice and coconut. Stirring slowly, sprinkle pudding mix into fruit mixture. Let stand 5 minutes. Pudding will set in fruit juice. Makes 6 1/2 cup servings.

Child's Party Favors

Edible Orange Favor: Have each child color a jack-o-lantern face on an orange with a black marker. If it's spring, draw a bunny face and add construction paper ears. Each child takes his creation home with him to eat.

Photo Favor: Take an instant photo of each child at the party. When it's time to go home, give each child his picture to take with him to remember the fun.

From Dian Thomas, *Today Tips for Easy Living* (Tucson, Arizona: H.P. Book).

Games

How to Plan a Successful Reunion

To be successful, a reunion must not only furnish the people who attend a good time, but must enable them to feel comfortable and at home. It must give them a genuinely joyful experience, send them away feeling they have made good use of their time and hoping they can come again.

The mere desire to have a reunion is not sufficient to make the event a success. You must select your activities and plan your events so they will actually affect people favorably.

How to Select Good Games

There are at least two ways of judging the games you plan to use. Do they "go off" as planned? Obviously a game is not good if it will not work. Whether it will work for you depends on the size of the crowd, the physical surroundings, such as size and shape of the area, the amount of running or moving about the players are required to do, and so on. All these things are more or less obvious. With a little thought you can select from a large number of games those that will work in your reunion and for your crowd. Read each game over carefully, picturing as you read just what would happen if your group should play it. You can thus select some games as useful and discard others as useless for your purposes. Plenty of outdoor games are found in the book *Double Fun* by Alma Heaton. Titles of books that include indoor games are found in the back of this book.

There is another kind of judgment you must pass on the

games you plan to use — a kind of judgment tht is often neglected because it is less obvious than the other. This judgment has to do with the mental — and sometimes even the physical — effect they have on the people who take part. Here are a few simple requirements that, in the opinion of the writer, are essential to games that can be called *successful* for church-centered reunions. These are not iron-clad rules; rather, they are goals to be attained.

Selecting the Right Game

Selecting suitable games and games that will have the kind of effect you desire is only one part of planning successful activities for reunions. An equally important part is arranging the games so the effect of the whole reunion will give folks a grand time and make them want to come again.

The first game to plan for the reunion is an activity that will give the first arrivals something interesting to do, make them forget their self-consciousness, and create within them the feeling that the party is to be spirited and interesting.

These activities must be easy to enter. People coming after a few others have started to play must be able to pick up the idea and join the group at once without a noticeable interruption. These games should introduce the family members to each other and be a time of sociability.

The following games and activities are given to suggest more fully what can be used for the first part of the reunion. Only five or six are needed, just enough to get the reunion started.

Tags or badges on which the family names are written and then pinned on their clothing give new family members a sense of belonging and help folks get acquainted. Each family has a different colored name tag.

What Are the Qualities of a Good Game?

1. It must allow people to feel at ease in playing. It should not embarrass them or make them feel foolish or ridiculous. A game that makes a fool of some individual or small group for the amusement of the others embarrasses those who are

the "goats" and makes others in the group feel uncomfortable and ill-at-ease for fear they may be the next victims.

2. The game should tend to make people forget themselves and should focus their attention on what they are doing. Things that require some amount of skill are most likely to accomplish this. Throwing darts at a target, tossing rings at a peg, and cooperating in some group activity that requires team work are examples.
3. The game should appeal to the good qualities in folks, rather than to their lower impulses. Putting a candy bar in the center of the room and having everybody rush for it at a given signal may result in an interesting grand scramble, but much else does not recommend it. Kissing games are in this class; they pervert emotions that are worthy of more discriminating tastes! Even very thoughtless persons will notice that some games stir a crowd to regular roughhousing and uncontrolled boisterousness, while other games seem to keep the crowd in better order.
4. The game should not cheapen or make fun of beautiful and sacred things of real virtues or standards. For instance, a good game would not make fun of love or marriage. Cheap jokes should have no place in your program, nor should suggestive and cheap parodies of beautiful songs or hymns. These things result in making the real song or real virtue seem foolish to those who have sung or heard the cheap words.

   On the other hand, the games you choose and the songs you sing at your party can be such that when folks remember them later, they will be rewarded with a rich and beautiful memory of the occasion when they learned them.

After everyone has arrived and become tired of free-play activities, the activity director should lead a game that helps the group assemble into one area. Relay races, sawdust scrambles, and competitive games are usually the most enjoyable games at this point. Several adults are needed to arrange age groups into starting lines; others are needed to be judges and to hand out prizes, match fathers against sons for competitive relays, and conduct dinner activities. The older folks are usually content to watch, especially if the relays are entertaining and well matched.

Mix up the groups of relatives with games that can be played by all ages. Young Chuck, who thought he had the makings of a chess champ, may find himself forced to the wall by Uncle Mark.

Institute a quiet time if the noise level gets deafening. Though you may be used to high-pitched voices and boisterous laughter, childless families or those with grown children are not. If the situation gets tense, gather all the youngsters together and play the pantomime game. No one can speak unless he says the magic phrase, "May I?" Everything else has to be done by gestures. The sudden cessation of sound will delight everyone.

Do you see anyone you know? Shall we stop or drive on? These are questions that might be going through the minds of relatives as they arrive. Unless they can see some action, they might start out with a negative attitude. Everyone wants to be where the action is and to feel comfortable and relaxed. At a canyon reunion, the activities could be several kinds of games: softball, volleyball, etc. These types of games not only interest a lot of people, but they can easily absorb new people as they arrive. The older folks are usually satisfied to visit with other family members and to work on family history.

The young might be reluctant to leave their parents for other activities. However, this shyness will not last long if the activity director for the reunion has planned for the young as well as for the older folks. Swings, frisbees, and other simple game equipment interest the young. Streams of water also catch their attention, so be sure to have an adult supervisor around at all times. If a cable with a pulley swing is tied between two trees, the young will love to swing between the trees. If there is a hillside close by, a rope can be tied to a nearby limb for the young to swing off the hill and back again.

If the reunion is held indoors, there could be name tags and a large paper tree on the wall that each person could sign; it's often fun for the youth to find which branch they belong to and write their games. For indoor reunions, it's important to find table games or indoor games that can be played by any number of people and ones that can absorb new players at any time. With minor changes in equipment, outdoor games such as softball, volleyball, or hockey can be modified so they can be played indoors. Often these modified outdoor games are more fun than actually playing them outdoors.

As relatives arrive at the reunion, they participate in easily organized, individual activities. The group usually scatters throughout the area, finding places to park and visiting with relatives. It may take an hour or two for all to arrive and get oriented with their surroundings.

How to Introduce a Game, Contest, or Race

1. Put the group in formation to play game.
2. Name it.
3. Demonstrate and explain it.
4. Start it.
5. Stop it while they want more.

Leaders should do the following:

1. Know the event thoroughly before attempting to teach it.
2. Complete all preparations for an event before attempting to introduce it.
3. Never attempt to explain anything until quiet and attention are absolute.
4. Make the play period continuously snappy and vigorous.
5. Develop the spirit of play and avoid the idea of work.
6. Look for backward, reticent members and try to get them into the game, but do not use force or get "hard boiled."
7. Never introduce a large number of new games at one time.
8. Play several games in one formation before changing formations.

9. Be ready to take over a party at any time or place.
10. Have a game in mind for every situation.

Outdoor Games

One of the first phases of the family reunion is to have a variety of activities set up as families arrive at the reunion. This is a good method as an opener to the reunion to get acquainted with each other.

For ***outdoor reunions,*** games can be set up on card tables with the following rules:

1. Have one skill game for every four persons to be present (card or bingo games).
2. Provide large numbers (1 to 25) for each game. Place a number on each table so that it can be seen.
3. Participants should progress from one game to another.
4. Participants may challenge each other in their favorite game.
S. Place a copy of rules by each game.

Games that can be used for *Outdoor Reunions*

Team sport activities (can be co-educational)

1. Volleyball
2. Softball
3. Badminton
4. Kickball

Activity games for small children

1. Zoo games
2. Treasure hunts
3. Nursery rhymes
4. Story telling
5. Name the animal, state, bird, or flower game
6. Sawdust scramble

Group relays

1. Tube races
2. Wheelbarrow races
3. Passing relays
4. Sack relays

Individual contests for all ages

1. Running races
2. Prizes given for places (first, second, third)
3. Prizes also for all who run

Pillow Free-for-All

When the seats of old pants wear out, cut the legs off and fill the legs with sponge rubber. Sew the ends together and you have a fighting pillow. (The pant legs will last longer if they are double thickness.)

Each participant holds one foot in the air and swings the pillow with one hand. When a player loses his balance and falls, he is eliminated from the game. The players must stay inside the designated area. The player who can keep from being eliminated is the winner.

Four-Way Tug-of-War

Find or purchase 12 feet of soft cotton rope and tie the ends together. Place four people inside, facing outward in four different directions. Place the belt across their stomachs for a four corner tug-of-war. Participants reach for a piece of candy placed directly in front of them about 6 feet away. The person to grab his piece of candy first is the winner and gets all four pieces of candy.

Rag Ball

Roll one half of an old towel up tight and tie a string around the middle, and you have a soft baseball. The ball is about 2 inches in diameter and 6 inches in length. Use a broomstick for the bat, and you will seldom knock the rag ball over a fence.

Circle Baseball

Drill a hole through the middle of an old softball. Place a rope through the hole and tie a knot on the end of the rope. Hold the free end of the rope in your hand and swing the ball in a circle as several participants try to hit it with sawed-off bats.

Soccer Baseball

Kicking a soccer ball can be as much fun as hitting a regular baseball. Use regular softball or baseball rules, but play only 4 innings for each team. This game can be played in a small area, and all ages can participate. You may want to modify the rules for small children or even make up your own game. Creating your own rules can be a lot of fun.

Pillow the King

Lay a 2x4 on the grass. Choose one player to be king. Any participant who can knock the king off the plank becomes the king himself.

Circle Jump Rope

Tie an old stocking filled with rags to a rope 10-15 feet long. Whirl it in a circle close to the ground and give everyone who wants a chance to jump the rope. When a player in the circle is hit with the sock, he takes his turn swinging the rope.

Two-Way Tug-of-War

Use webbing that is 2 inches wide and 6 feet long. Sew the ends together to make a loop. Participants can crawl through it, jump over it, neck pull, or ankle pull for a tug-of-war.

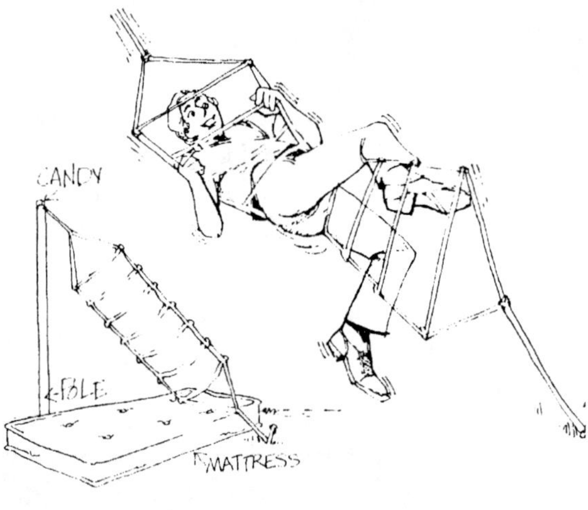

Jacob's Rope Ladder

Make a rope ladder about 15 feet long. Fasten the ropes together at each end of the ladder. Tie one end of it to the top of a pole and secure the other end to a peg placed in the ground. Place a candy bar at the top of the pole. The person

who is able to climb the ladder and grab the candy bar without turning upside down is the winner.

Tarzan Jump Swing

Find a sloping hill or a bank. Tie one end of a strong 20-foot rope to a tree limb. Tie a large knot in the other end of the rope and use it as a seat. Hold the dangling end of the rope in your hands about 3 feet up from the knot; move several feet backwards, and then jump onto the knot seat. See how far out you can swing.

Sawdust Scramble

Place several pennies, candy chews, or gum in a pile of sawdust or wood shavings. All children of the same age line up five feet away. At the starting signal, they run to the sawdust and hunt for candy. They may keep all they find.

Each age group takes its turn, with more candy and more sawdust added with each age. Last of all, the fathers take their turn. All will climb over each other to get to the sawdust. The boys get a real charge watching their fathers act like boys.

Multiple-Legged Relay Race

To make large elastic bands for some of the relays, an old inner tube may be used. Cut the tube in two-inch strips by cutting from the inside of the tube across to the outside.

For a three-legged race, place the rubber band around the inside legs of two people standing side by side; these couples will have a lot of fun trying to coordinate their steps to win the race. This may be extended to a five- or seven-legged race by placing more participants together.

Human Wheelbarrow Race

One participant of a team places his hands on the ground (in a push-up position) and his partner steps between his legs and lifts him up by the knees. On signal, the human wheelbarrow is "pushed" to the goal line. At this point the pusher and the wheelbarrow change places and run back to the starting point.

When the clan is tired of physical activities, it's time to rest. A good opportunity occurs at this point for the program. It's a nice change.

Indoor Games

Who Am I?

As the relatives arrive, pin the name of a family member on the back of each. Instruct him to move around the group trying to discover the name by asking questions. When he correctly identifies the person, he pins the name in front.

Crazy Handshakes

All players start walking around when music starts to play. When it stops, the leader calls out the handshake they are to use, and the players turn, introduce themselves, and execute the specified handshake. These are some handshakes that might be fun:

Chinese Handshake: Shake one's own hand and bow three times.

Paul Bunyan: Grasp one's own right thumb in left fist, hold other person's right hand with own right hand (what remains), and saw away, saying "timber!"

Model-T Handshake: Grasp opposite's right hand and turn it like cranking.

Grandpa: Stroke one's beard.

Father: Shave.

Son: Comb one's hair.

Any person failing to perform his action in time changes places with *it*. There should be one *it* for each ten players in the circle. This may be repeated with grandma, knitting; mother, darning; daughter, sewing.

Suggested Activities

Tour of family homes, cemetery, and other things associated with family

Writing contest

Song contest

Name tag contest

Vacation contest (cheapest, etc.)

Display of grandparent's belongings (tools, furniture, etc.)

Take Advantage of What the Area Has to Offer

Parks

Lakes

Fishing

Hiking

Boats

Golf

Water skiing

Arts and crafts

White elephant auction

Sunday School

Testimony meeting

Get-Acquainted Musical Mixers

Popularity

Women on inside, men on outside, march in single file in opposite directions. When the whistle blows, the women about face, hook on the men's arms and march with them — extras go to the center. When the whistle blows again, women march in opposite directions. If there are more than two women to one man, let a woman get on each side of a man. If there are many times more women, let them fall in behind them as seven women on each man's coattail.

Find Your Father and Stoop

March a double circle, girls on the outside, boys on the inside. The leader of the game blows a whistle, which is a signal for the inside circle to reverse and march in the opposite direction. The whistle is blown a second time, and all players in the inside circle make a dash to join their fathers. As families are rejoined, they must clasp hands and stoop. The last family to stoop is eliminated from the game, and the marching is resumed as before. When only two families remain, the one that stoops first is the winner of the game.

As You Were with Families

Families march in single file. The leader calls directions for the group: "Girls inside, boys outside." "Girls in front of boys." "Halt, girls turn to face boys." "Then grand right and left." They alternate, the girls moving one direction and the boys in another, until the leader shouts, "As you were." At this command, each person must find his family and line up ready to march. Last one to line up is the loser and has to pay a forfeit by pulling on a slum, etc.

Musical Madhouse

Each grandfather gathers his descendants into one single circle. When the music begins, all march around. Leader suddenly blows a number of blasts on the whistle (example: four). Players then stop marching and form small circles of four with hands joined. Those left out of a small circle must stand in center until the next signal. One blast starts the march again in a single circle. The next signal may be six blasts, at which circles of six are formed. Whenever circles are being formed, those in the center try to join one. Vary the whistle blasts: four, six, three, etc. This may also be played with all families in one large circle.

Circle Introductions

One person starts the game by going up to another person and introducing himself. Then he and that person go in opposite directions to two other people and repeat the formality. As soon as a person in the circle receives an introduction from one of the people in the center, he leaves the circle and joins those in the center. The introductions continue until the leader blows a whistle; then all the center players scamper back to place. The last one back starts the game the second time.

Check the book *Double Fun* for more outdoor games. The price list is in the back of this book.

Reunion Songs
(fill in blanks with your name)

Tune: Battle Hymn of the Republic

As a band of ______ descendants,
    We have met to celebrate
And honor our ancestors,
    Fathers grand and fathers great;
They were leaders with the foremost,
    Who came west to found a state.
All honor to their name.

Chorus
Onward, Onward, each descendant;

Make our name shine forth resplendent;
Every _______ independent,
And glorify our name.

We want to get acquainted
and to really know our kin
And hear about our ancestors so
we can honor them.
We want to gather names and
dates for genealogy.
Please help us in this cause.

Not only do we talk and hear,
we have activities:
Sports and relays, active games
of all varieties.
The old, the young, the in between
can all join in the fun —
A challenge to your skills.

Smiles

There are families that make us happy.
There are families that make us blue.
There are families that steal away the teardrops
As the sunbeams steal away the dew.
There are names that have a tender meaning,
Relatives we love and see.
The reunions that fill my life with sunshine
Are the _______ my family!

Tune: Yankee Doodle

We meet today to celebrate
In honor of the _____,
Who help to make our country great
By being born in ______.

Chorus — after last and first verse
______ glorify our name.
Let it never shame us.
Everyone get in the game
and help to make us famous.

When all the _____ come to town,
You think it is a nation.
I never knew the world could hold
So gol'darn much relation.

The _____ learns arithmetic
Without a bit of trying;
At adding they are very quiet,
But quicker multiplying.

The _____ grow so very tall
That some of them are taller
Than others who are not so small
And others who are smaller.

The early_____ loved the farm
And raising pigs and chickens,
But such a life has lost its charm
For some who raise the dickens.

Beans, chips and punch and cupcakes, too,
For this we "get-together."
Please join us in our fun and games;
It may be now or never!

Here we are; we came to town.
Listen to the laughter;
The ones we miss, not with us now,
We'll join in the hereafter!

Come back and visit your home town —
All families are invited;
New friends and members have been found,
So let's get reunited!

Tune: The Caissons Go Rolling Along

Over hill, over dale,
We have hit the dusty trail
As those cousins go rolling along.
"Counter march! Right about!"
Hear those aunts and uncles shout
While those cousins go rolling along.

Chorus
For it's
Hi, hi, hee in the _____ family.
Call off your children loud and strong.
(Call off your first name)
And where ever we go, you will always know
That those cousins are rolling along.
(keep 'em rolling)
That those cousins are rolling along.

Tune: Pretty Baby

Well, we'd like to get together;
That's why we invited you.
Welcome _____, welcome _____,
We'll have fun and games and prizes,
And perhaps a laugh or two
Welcome _____, welcome _____,
Won't you come along and sing a song
And tell a joke for me?
We'll be happy as can be.
And we'll meet right here throughout the years
To share our families.
Well you _____ — Alright!

Tune: Popcorn Popping on the Apricot Tree

We looked out the window, and what did we see?
Cousins growing on the family tree!
We all gather once a year
To be with family from far and near.
We like to visit and stay real close
To all the people we love the most.
So here we are again,
Happy with our kin.
(We've got) cousins growing onto
Family tree!

Tune: It's a Small World

There is just one family for you and me,
and we'll love each through eternity.
We will stand side by side,
Full of love and family pride.
We're a family after all.
Heritage from days now past,
Great traditions that will last,
Loyalty that's strong and fast,
We're a family after all.

We are here today for some family fun
To be unified now with everyone.
We will all do our part,
Bringing joy to every heart.
We're a family after all.

We're a family after all
Every member large and small,
Young and old we love them all.
We're a family after all.

Tune: Cougar Fight Song

Rise and shout our family is out on the road to our reunion.
Rise and sing what joy it will bring to gather all our stakes of Zion.
On we go, the young and the old,
Meeting all their sons and daughters.
As we join in song, in praise of God, we all are strong.
We'll meet and play and laugh all the day,
So glad that we could be here with you.

Tune: You're a Grand Old Flag

(About our family)
We're a singing family, and we're proud as can be
To belong to the _____ Family Tree.
Of our heritage, we love to sing
Of blessings the gospel does bring.
Our work with bees makes us sweet if you please.
We all know where we belong.
We'll all stick together in all kinds of weather
Is the name of our family song.

(To our relatives)
You're a grand family, and we're proud of our tree.
Uncles, aunts, cousins too, we love to see.
We are proud of you; you're staunch and true.
Together, we make quite a few.
_____, _____ we do proudly acclaim.
We are glad we belong to you.
Well stand together firm and strong
And honor the _____ name.

Tune: Welcome, Welcome Sabbath Morning

Welcome, welcome dearest family,
We're so glad we all are here —
Fathers, mothers, aunts, and uncles,
Every family member dear.

Games and contests to entertain us,
All the food that we can eat,
And renewing family acquaintance,
We know our family can't be beat.

Welcome, welcome happy family.
We are here to join the fun,
For we cherish our relations.
We're so glad that you are ONE!

We all have fun together, honor to our name
And you again next year to glorify the same.
It makes us all much happier for our attendance here.
We hope you'll make an effort to attend again next year.

Tune: Pack Up Your Troubles

Pack up your family in your own R.V.
And come, come, come.
Here's to the family we want to see.
Just call your day's work done.
What's the use of worrying?
We're off to have some fun!
So pack up your family in your old R.V.
And come, come, come.

Tune: Shall the Youth of Zion Falter

Shall the _____ family falter in meeting once a year?
While time moves on so quickly, shall we forget our
Kin so dear?
NO!

Chorus
True to the faith that our forefathers left us,
True to the name that we cherish, each of us,
All God's commands we'll understand.
Faithful and true we join hand in hand.

Shall the _____ find excuses to seek their kindred dead?
With the temples all around us shall we stay apart instead?
NO!
Chorus
Shall the _____ service in behalf of fellow men?
Shall they strive to teach their families to reach the eternal plan?
YES!
Chorus
Shall the _____ stand united in the love of our true God?
While the world is yet divided will we grasp the family rod?
YES!
Chorus

Tune: You Are My Sunshine

You are my family —
My wonderful family.
You make me happy
When you are near.
You'll never know dear
How much I love you
Or how I'll always hold you dear.

Tune She'll Be Comin' Round the Mountain

Oh, we're going to a reunion, Yessiree!
Oh, we're going to a reunion, Yessiree!
Oh, we're going to a reunion.
There is nothing like a reunion.
Oh, we're going to a Reunion, Yessiree!

Oh, they'll all come out and meet us when we come.
Oh, they'll all come out and meet us when we come.
Oh, they'll all come out and meet us.
They'll hug and kiss, and greet us.
Oh, they'll all come out and meet us when we come.

Oh, there'll be many happy faces when we come.
Oh, there'll be many happy faces when we come.
Oh, there'll be many happy faces
Food and drinks by the cases.
Oh, there'll be many happy faces when we come.

Oh, there's nothing like a reunion, Yessiree!
Oh, there's nothing like a reunion, Yessiree!
Oh, there's nothing like a reunion
To assure a family union.
Oh, there's nothing like a reunion, Yessiree!

Tune: Mormon Sunday School

Young folks, old folks, everybody come
Join the _____ family and have a lot of fun.
Bring your children and your pets —
Your worries leave behind —
Cause we're gonna play and visit,
And of course we're gonna dine.

Well, if your name is _____ and even if it's not,
Come listen to the story of the heritage.
Father _____ was a fine man, brave and loyal, strong and true
With a testimony of the gospel that he knew.

Patience, love and understanding guided Mother _____ way,
And the memory of her charity lives within us today.
Together out in Utah a family they grew —
Fifteen healthy, husky boys, eleven daughters, too.

Now we've gathered here together as a family group today
To get to know each other so that we can truly say
That the glorious tribe of _____ is on the earth to stay.
So let's all shout together in a loud and clear "Hurray!"

Tune: Battle Hymn of the Republic

Mine eyes have seen the future
Of the _____ family.

We all have great ambitions
In our genealogy,
And with united effort
We will form a family tree
As we go marching on.

Chorus: Glory, glory hallelujah…The family marches on.

We've gathered here together
To help to push the work along,
Rejoice in real achievement
In our music, verse, and song.
And in the distant future
We will join the heavenly throng
As we go marching on.

Tune: Daisy, Daisy

Reunion, reunion,
It's family gathering time
From lands close and lands afar
To honor our family line.
With sisters, brothers, cousins,
Grandparents, aunts, and uncles,
We'll share our life, increase our love,
And find joy in our family.

Tune: Hello Dolly

Hello cousins, well hello cousins.
It's so nice to be together once again.
We'll all have fun, cousins,
And play games, dozens,
To see if we can end up lasting friends.

We've got the name, cousins,
And the fame, cousins.
So all join in and keep it rolling on.
YES!

We're the best cousins
In the west, cousins.
Stick together, we'll keep rolling on.
Hang together, we'll keep growing.
All together, join our happy throng.

Tune: This Land is Your Land

This clan is your clan
This clan is my clan
From Grandpa _____,
Who was a fine man.
He and his good wife
And kin before them
Gave us a heritage of love.

Our pioneer fold
Came cross this country
With backs and feet sore
And without money
To settle Zion
And live the gospel
And leave us a heritage of love.

They showed us wisdom
And faith and courage,
So let's unite now
And do not worry,
But carry forward
The work they started
And earn us our heritage of love.

Tune: Improve the Shining Moments

Grandfather loved his family.
He gathered them around.
It's here we grew together.
Come to the country-farm
Reunions where they started to strengthen family ties
To know each other better and to enrich our lives.

We love to have reunions
To meet and greet our kin
With programs and entertainment and food fit for a king.
If we had no relation, how lonely it would be.
Our lives would be so empty
If our folks we could not see.

Tune: Dearie

Genealogy Song by Janie Thompson

(Setting: Two very discouraged spirits up in heaven discussing their plight)

She: Dearie, do you believe the folks on earth will ever begin
Tracing the knee that eve are in...
I am getting slightly impatient,
For so many years have passed by.

He: You can say that again, my dearie —
Our sons and daughters really
Don't seem to care if we...sit up here indefinitely;
Their hesitating just keeps us waiting.

She: And dearie, you're much older than I...

She: Dearie, how well I do recall, way back in the good old days
When Abraham Lincoln freed the slaves —
You would think that our dear descendants
Would try to free you and I... (poetic license)

He: Yes, I must agree, but dearie,
Just look at all those young folks
Running round in a great big fuss,
Doing everything else but helping us.
Dearie, life is dreary...and there's just one reason.
They're not realizing...we need baptizing —
It's our salvation they do deny.

She: Dearie, if we could only just...
Inspire Peg and Frank and Sue to do their genealogy, too...
Young folks always leave it to others,
Like old Uncle Ned or Aunt Vye.

He: And that just won't do, you know, dearie.
If they would only just...
Try to do a little bit, they soon would get the spirit of it.

Both: Dearie, it's no theory., so you just wait until THEY DIE!
Then they'll be sorry, they can't get to glory (say it like sorry).
Without us they can't climb very high...no ESCALATORS —
They need us, too; that's no lie.

Tag Ending: Now folks, we don't want to bore you
But we implore you—get out and hustle
New names to rustle.
We're out here grieving...we need reprieving.
Give geneal—o—gy work a a try...RIGHT NOW!

Personal History Guide

Answer the following questions in complete sentences. Some questions may take several sentences or paragraphs to answer. Answer them with as much detail as you like. Add or delete questions as needed. After the questionnaire is finished, you will have a personal history.

1. Where and when were you born?
2. Who are your parents? When and where were they born and married?
3. Do you have brothers and sisters? Who are they and when/where were they born?
4. Where did you live when you were small?
5. What are your first memories of home?
6. What are some things you might share about the memories of your parents, brothers and sisters, or home life when you were small?
7. Can you remember going to church when you were small?
8. When were you baptized? By whom? By whom wree you confirmed?
9. Where did you go to elementary school?
10. Did you have any special interests or hobbies during your elementary years?
11. What are some special grade school activities in which you participated?
12. What are some of the special family activities you remember during these years?
13. Where and when did you go to Jr. High School?
14. What are some of your memories of these school years?
15. (Males) When were you ordained to the Aaronic Priesthood? Who ordained you and when?
16. What memories do you have of church activities? Sunday School? Mutual? Scouts?
17. Where and when did you go to high school?
18. Did you participate in any extra curricular activities? Explain.
19. Who were some of your special friends during your teen years?
20. Did you have any memorable experiences that taught you important lessons or that helped shape your life?
21. Were you active in church during your teen years?
22. Who were some of the special people that influenced your life for good?

23. What were some of the things that increased your testimony of the gospel?
24. What are some of the enjoyable things your family did together during your teen years?
23. Did you have any hobbies or special interests during these years? Explain.
26. Did you work at any part-time or full-time jobs during your teen years?
27. Did you graduate from high school? When?
28. Did you go into the service? To college? On a mission? Get married? Go to work? Explain.
29. What special experiences did you have during the above occupation?
30. When, where, and to whom were you married?
31. What are some of the special memories about your marriage?
32. Where did you live after you were married?
33. What were some of the challenges and problems you faced during early married life?
34. How did you/your partner make a living? Where have you/your partner worked since?
35. How did you/your partner come to choose your occupation?
36 How many children do you have? Where and when were they born? Describe the coming of each child and what each one was like.
37. What were some of the special things you did as a family with your children?
38. What were some of the projects you worked on together as a family?
39. What were some of the things you did to teach your children the gospel?
40. Explain any special or faith-promoting experiences you have experienced in your family.
41. What callings and responsibilities have you had in the church since your marriage?
42. What callings has your partner had in the church?
43. Have you had any faith-promoting experiences with respect in these callings?

44. How have these responsibilities blessed and enriched your family and home?

45. Have you engaged in any community or civic service activities?

46. How have these experiences broadened youf and your family?

47. What special activities have your children been engaged in?

48. What special counsel or message of love would you like to give to your children and posterity?

49. What faith or character-building experiences would you like to share with your posterity?

50. Share your testimony of the gospel of Jesus Christ.

Missionary Reunions

Missionary reunions could be held every year at General Conference time. All members from the mission field should be invited.

During the program many will want to know what has happened in the mission field since they left.

Social activities should be held. Missionaries can visit while dancing. A professional square dance caller could be invited to direct the program.

Refreshments, a buffet dinner, or assigned pot-luck dinner could be served.

Missionaries could bring pictures (of their missionary experiences, of their families, etc.) to share with others. Projectors and screens (or walls) could be provided for such activities.

Class Reunions

Class reunions are where old people get together to see who is falling apart. Most of the time spent at the first reunion should be devoted to visiting, programs, and eating. If the class has not seen each other for a long time, many will not recognize their classmates, so introductions should be made.

If classes meet together every year or every five or ten years, more time could be spent in entertainment, and an activity such as square dancing would be appropriate. Perhaps one of the group can direct the square dancing or other activities. If not, some professional could be hired to entertain and direct the square dancing or other activities.

During the program, those attending should be brought up-to-date on what has happened since last roll call. Class reunions could be held in the home town, maybe at the old school house. School songs could be sung. Former cheerleaders could lead the group in the school cheers. Prizes could be given for achievements such as the largest or smallest families, who has traveled the farthest distance, one with the most children or grandchildren, one who has changed least, each of the teachers, the one who can sing the school song from memory, etc. Use your imagination to come up with other ideas for activities, prizes, etc.

How to Know You're Growing Older

Everything hurts, and what doesn't hurt doesn't work.

You feel like that night after, and you haven't been anywhere.

You get winded playing checkers.

Your mind makes contracts that your body can't meet.

A dripping faucet causes an uncontrollable urge.

Your back goes out more often than you do.

The little gray-haired lady you help across the street is your wife.

You look forward to a dull evening.

You turn out the lights for economic reasons rather than romantic ones.

When you don't care how long you stay out as long as you're home by nine o'clock.

You attract widespread attention from the bathroom mirror.

You get exhausted by wrestling with your conscience.

You'd rather not have a good time than get over it.

You feel fit as a fiddle but bulge like a bass violin.

Tripping the light fantastic becomes less light and more fantastic.

You no longer care where your wife wants to go as long as you don't have to go with her.

Your memory is shorter, your experience longer, your stamina lower, and your forehead higher.

Your knees buckle but your belt won't.

You suspect your grandkids are doing what you did at their age.

She puts on her bra backwards and finds it fits and looks better that way.

You discover that your waterbed broke and then realize that you don't have a water bed.

At class reunions, you call each other boys and girls.

—Earnest Kirby

Sample Invitation

JOSEPH SMITH, SR. FAMILY REUNION
Independence, Missouri 1973
August 16, 17, 18
Hosted by the Descendants of
Joseph Smith, Jr.

RECEPTION AND REGISTRATION
OPENING SESSION FRIDAY MORNING
August 17, 9:30 a.m.

HYMN Oh Beautiful for Spacious Skies . . . . .No. 98

INVOCATION

STATEMENTS OF WELCOME

Descendant of Joseph Smith, III
Descendant of Alexander Smith
Descendant of David H. Smith

STATEMENTS OF RESPONSE

Descendant of Hyrum Smith
Descendant of Samuel Smith
Descendant of Catherine Smith Salisbury

FILM *Seeds of Greatness*
produced by Buddy Youngreen

INTERVIEW OF AUTHOR PEARL WILCOX
by Anina Larsen Mackay
With the Latter-day Saints on the Mission Frontier

BENEDICTION

• • • • • •

FRIDAY AFTERNOON SESSION
1:30 to 3:30 p.m.

INVOCATION

STRING ENSEMBLE . . . . .The Floyd Mengel Family
(Beattrice - piano; Leslie - cello; Dana - violin)

Einekleinacht (Mozart) . . . . .by the ensemble

Concerto No. 1, 1st movement (Saint-Saen) . . . . .by Leslie Mengel

PRESENTATION — Joseph Fielding Smith, son of Hyrum
By Dr. Leonard Arrington, L.D.S. Church Historian

HYMN These Things Shall Be a Loftier Race . . . . .No. 202

BENEDICTION

• • • • • •

(Additional activities listed, as above, for each succeeding day of the reunion.)

Example of an Indoor Reunion

9:00 a.m. Opening Song ....page 71

Opening Prayer

Introduction and Welcome, S. Blaine Willes, Stake President

Speaker, Susan Hill, Director of Youth Program, LDS Genealogical Library, Salt Lake City

10:00 a.m. "Could It Happen to You?" ....a play

by Edmund Crowley, directed by Lynette Zemp

10:35 a.m. Get on the Family-Go-Round! Earn a "Bug!"

Round I It's All in the Book: Your Book of Remembrance . .*Stella Hatch*

Round II Organizing Your Family ....*Jonathan M. Chamberlain*

Round III Four Generations of Your Family ....*Loretta Bamgartner*

12:20 pm **BOX LUNCH** (Give donations of $1 or more to Sharon West Stake Special Interest project, coordinated by Ethal Butler.)

KNOW YOUR PEDIGREE CONTEST

OPEN TO ALL AGES

WIN A PRIZE

1:00 p.m.

Round IV It's Fun to Find — Some Basic Steps ....Bill Sidwell

Round V Personal Diaries and Histories ....Evelyn Schiess

Round VI Family Fun and Recreation ....Alma Heaton

2:45pm

Round VII The Genealogy Song by Janie Thompson

FILM Family Recreation by Alma Heaton

3:15 p.m. Awards and Prizes

3:30p.m. Closing Prayer

KEEP THE FAMILY-GO-ROUND GOING

FAMILY GROUP SCHEDULES

Please participate in the Family-Go-Round in the following sequence:

Family A (Blue Tags) I, II, III, Box Lunch IV, V, VI, VII

Family B (Red Tags) II, III, I, Box Lunch V, VI, IV, VII

Family C (Yellow Tags) III, I, II, Box Lunch VI, IV, V, VII

Special Stake Advisors — Stella Hatch, Evelyn Schiess, Bill Sidwell

Stake High Council Representative for Genealogy and Temple work — Jon Chamberlain

Example of an Outdoor Reunion Program

COX FAMILY REUNION NOTICE

Date:	August 13-16
Where:	Flat Canyon and Fairview, Utah
Who:	All descendants of Jonathan Upham Cox, especially descendants of the three children who came to Utah: Fredrick Walker Cox, Orville Sutherland Cox, and Mary Elizabeth Cox Whiting. This reunion will honor three children of Orville S. Cox: Tryphena C. Sidwell, 9m, Amasa B. Cox, 10m, and Philena C. Esplin, 11m.

AGENDA

Fri., Aug. 13	Set up camp at Flat Canyon, visit, get acquainted
6:30 p.m.	Fireside program honoring Tryphena Sidwell, by her descendants
Sat., Aug. 14	
Sun., Aug. 15,	
10:00 a.m.	Business meeting, Fairview, probably in the South Ward Chapel; program honoring Amasa B. Cox, by his descendants
6:30 p.m.	Dance and good time at Flat Canyon
9:00 a.m.	Priesthood meeting at Flat Canyon
10:00 a.m.	Sunday School and Sacrament Meeting at Flat Canyon (You can visit at the Fairview Wards, if you desire.)
Monday, Aug 16	Temple session at 11:25 a.m. at the Salt Lake Temple.

Some of the cousins have difficulty with the altitude of Flat Canyon, so the presidents have decided to hold the Saturday meetings at Fairview this year.

Don't forget the camping sticker now required for the forest camps if you plan on camping at Flat Canyon Campground. The Cox property is adjacent to the camp, and if you just come up for the programs, you can park outside the campground. Please come early Thursday, if possible, to help preserve the campground for the Coxes.

WHAT: The LANGSTON FAMILY REUNION

WHEN: JUNE 14, 1969

(Those who can are welcome to come Friday evening and camp overnight or stay 'til Sunday.)

WHERE: OAK CITY CANYON (Mts. east of Delta)

(The main part of the canyon just as you cross the creek has been reserved. There are drinking water, restrooms, plenty of room for trailers and tents, and a large pavilion we can use.)

TIME: 12 o'clock noon — Lunch (This is left up to each family, depending on if they want to eat before or after the business meeting but be to the meeting)

1 p.m. BUSINESS MEETING

(Don't let this title, "business meeting," scare you. We would like every person, young, old, in between, or otherwise interested in making these reunions a success, to be there to voice opinions and help plan future reunions. This is the place to make your wants and wishes known.)

AGENDA

Activities of all kinds are being planned for all day. There will be a 'supervised' hike for all those who want to lest their climbing legs.

SPORTS of all kinds — something for everyone: SOFTBALL, VOLLEYBALL, HORSESHOE PITCHING, BADMINTON, CHINESE CHECKERS, MONOPOLY — and we will even throw in a card game if that's what you want. They say there are even a few fish in the creek.

COME PREPARED TO MINGLE WITH YOUR RELATIVES, TO HAVE A GOOD TIME AND GET TO KNOW EACH OTHER!!!

Saturday afternoon there will be a "Community Hot Dog Roast." Please bring your own hot dogs and buns and furnish a salad, chips, etc., to share with everyone else. Punch will be furnished for the group.

PLAN TO JOIN THE FAMILY

ENJOY THE DAY OR WEEKEND

(Whichever one you choose!)

REMEMBER THE DATE

June 14,1969

Get-Acquainted Games

Find Your Relatives

Find someone...

Related to you only though marriage ____________________

Whose last name is the original family name ______________

Under ten ____________________________________

Who knew your mom or dad when they were kids _________

Over sixty ____________________________________

Whom you have never met before____________________

Born the closest to the place you were born______________

Who enjoys doing genealogy _______________________

Who has been married less than one year ______________

Married more than thirty years _____________________

Attending college ______________________________

Who can tell you where your grandma was born __________

Who is a musician______________________________

Who traveled far to come here _____________________

Who is an athlete ______________________________

Who is the youngest in the family___________________

Who was at the last reunion _______________________

Who served a United States mission__________________

You have not seen for years _______________________

Who has been in the service _______________________

Who ran out of gas within the last year ______________

Genealogy

Fill in the blanks.

1. When a woman marries, the man to whom she is married is her _____.
2. The local checkers who inspect genealogical data to be sent in are _____ _____.
3. To be _____ means that you enter a body here on earth.
4. Nation _____
5. For the living to be _____ for themselves or for the dead, they must be immersed in water.
6. The _____ is the last name of the family.
7. Area containing several towns and perhaps one or more cities _____
8. Our first names are our _____.
9. To be _____ is to receive the ordinances in the temple that prepare us for eternal marriage.
10. Opposite of single _____
11. Information pertaining to temple work done for the dead _____
12. Offspring _____
13. Spouse (female) _____
14. Similar to a city _____
15. Many of our ancestors are _____ in churchyards.
16. To be _____ means to be given a name.
17. Information pertaining to your family is found on the _____ _____ _____.
18. The official record-gathering organization of the Church _____ _____
19. Progenitor _____
20. Opposite of born _____

KEY

1. Husband 2. Ward examiners 3. Body 4. Country 5. Baptized
6. Surname 7. County 8. Given names 9. Endowed 10. Married
11. Temple ordinance data 12. Children 13. Wife 14. Town 15. Buried
16. Christened 17. Family group record 18. Genealogical Society
19. Ancestor 20. Died

Family Reunion Pre-Opener

A. Fill in the blanks by unscrambling the words at the end of the sentences. (The underlined letters are not always the first letter in the word.)

B. Write the underlined letters in order of appearance at the bottom of the page.

KEY

1. _____ are eternal. (afmilsie)
2. If someone tells a funny joke, you _____. (glauh)
3. You can't have a family without a _____ and a father. (thomer)
4. Father _____ that I go to the reunion. (nsitsis)
5. "_____ one another." (eolv)
6. _____ are short plays. (stiks)
7. A talent show provides _____. (retnatieenntm)
8. We sing _____ in church. (snsog)
9. Everyone likes to play _____. (smage)
10. _____ are for young and old people. (neinsour)
11. Family reunions should be held once a _____. (reya)
12. If you chance to meet a frown, change it for a _____. (milse)
13. _____ should be involved at reunions. (royeneve)
14. Players who win the games will receive _____. (sripez)
15. _____ are mandatory at all reunions. (fershrestemn)
16. All families should provide five minutes of _____ on the program. (letant)
17. _____ include aunts, uncles, grandparents, etc. (laetrevis)
18. We _____ when we're together. (claiisoze)
19. _____ are handed down from generation to generation. (draistiont)
20. Man made _____ when he walked on the moon. (sithyro)

1. Families 2. Laugh 3. Mother 4. Insists 5. Love 6. Skits
7. Entertainment 8. Songs 9. Games 10. Reunions 11. Year
12. Smile 13. Everyone 14. Prizes 15. Refreshments 16. Talent
17. Relatives 18. Socialize 19. Traditions 20. History

Genealogy

Instructions. Tell what each of the following are to you.

1. Your father's only uncle's brother's father
2 Your aunt's mother's father's only daughter
3. Your mother's nephew's sister's father
4 Your brother's son's sister's father
5. Your sister-in-law's father-in-law's wife
6. Your sister's father's stepson's mother's husband
7. Your aunt's father's only grandchild
8. Your brother-in-law's wife's grandfather's wife
9. Your father's father's daughter's son
10. The grandson of the only son of your mother's mother-in-law

Answers to Genealogy

1. Great-Grandfather 2. Grandmother 3. Uncle 4. Brother

5. Mother 6. Father 7. Me or You 8. Grandmother 9. Cousin

10. Nephew

Skits

Reputation

Characters: Judge, Sheriff, Irishman

Scene: Courtroom

(As the scene opens, the Judge is addressing the Irishman before the bar.)

Judge: Now, sir, have you anyone in the court who can vouch for your character?

Irishman: Oh, the Sheriff there. He can.

Sheriff: Why, I don't even know this man.

Irishman: Observe, your Honor. I've lived twelve years in this county, and the Sheriff doesn't even know me.

Absentmindedness

Characters: Man, Conductor

Scene: On a train

(As the scene opens, the man is reading.)

Conductor: Your ticket, sir.

Man: Oh, yes. Just a moment. (He searches in his wallet, pocket, etc.)

Conductor: (He waits patiently, then says again) Sir…

Man: (Interrupts.) It must be here. (Searches.) Here, let me check my other pockets.

Conductor: Now don't be upset, sir. You ride with us quite regularly. We know you have your ticket. Why…

Man: (Interrupts again.) Of course I do. Here, let me look in my wallet again.

Conductor: But, sir…

Man: Maybe it's in my book.

Conductor: But sir, we're sure you have your ticket. When you find it, just mail it to the company.

Man: (Exploding) I know I have it! But what I want to know is where in the world am I going?

Double Trouble

Characters: Mrs. White, Policeman

Scene: Mrs. White's kitchen

(As the scene opens, Mrs. White is calling to the police.)

Mrs. White: (after dialing the number) Hello, hello! Police Department? Can you please help me? There's a skunk in our basement and the smell is terrible, and I don't know how to get him out. What will I do?

Policeman: (whose voice is heard over the loud speaker) Just follow my instructions, lady, and you can have him out in no time. Skunks like bread, so make a trail of bread crumbs from the basement to the yard and wait for the skunk to follow it outside.

Mrs. White: Crumbs of bread and make a trail with it. Okay. (She rushes to the bread box and gets bread, makes crumbs and rushes out calling, "Kitty, Kitty, Kitty." In a few moments she rushes back in and dashes for the phone and again dials the Police Department.)

Mrs. White: Hello, hello! Police Department? I did just what you told me to do. And now I've got two skunks in my basement.

Would You Believe

Character: Mother, Young Son Johnny

Scene: Living room

(As the scene opens, the young son enters from Sunday School.)

Johnny: Hi Mom!

Mother: Johnny, come and tell me what you learned in Sunday School today.

Johnny: Well, our teacher told us about when Heavenly Father sent Moses behind the enemy lines to rescue the Israelites from the Egyptians. And when they came to the Red Sea, well, Moses called for the engineers to build a pontoon bridge. After they had all crossed, they looked back and saw the Egyptian tanks coming. Quick as a flash, Moses radioed headquarters over his walkie-talkie to send bombers to blow up the bridge, and he saved the Israelites.

Mother: Now, Johnny, is that really the way your teacher told that story?

Johnny: Well not exactly. But if I told it her way, you'd never believe it.

The Path to Heaven

Characters: Preacher, Jimmy

Scene: Any street

(As the scene opens, Jimmy is selling newspapers on the corner when approached by a preacher.)

Preacher: Would you please tell me the way to the post office?

Jimmy: Down this street three blocks and turn to the left.

Preacher: Thank you, sonny. Do you know who I am?

Jimmy: Nope.

Preacher: I'm the famous preacher who is holding a revival over in the big tabernacle. If you will come to my meeting tonight, I will show you the way to heaven.

Jimmy: Aw, go on. You don't even know the way to the post office.

Time to Switch Partners

Characters: Mother, Jane.

Scene: The living room

(As the scene opens, Mother is sitting in an easy chair knitting. Jane comes rushing in.)

Jane: Mother, I've just got to have $75 for some new clothes. I've had six dates with Bill since I started college, and I've worn all the new dresses I got to start school. I have a date with him next weekend, and I must have a new dress.

Mother: Well, dear, we can't afford any new dresses. Get a new boyfriend and start over again.

BANG! BANG!

Characters: Sam, Bill

Scene: In the woods

(As the scene opens, Sam and Bill come in from opposite sides of the stage. Bill is supposedly carrying a gun. As they back into each other, Bill whirls and fires... Bang!)

Sam: You got me pal! (He doesn't fall. Bill fires again.)

Sam: You got me pal! (He still doesn't fall.)

Bill: If I got you, why don't you fall?

(Sam runs to the side of the stage and drags his friend on.)

Sam: I didn't say you got me; I said you got me pal.

Terrific Date

Characters: Fred, Bill

(As the scene opens, Fred and Bill are talking to each other.)

Fred: I had a terrific date last night. Blonde, really gorgeous. After the dance, we went out and parked by the lake. I asked her for a kiss. She said she would if I'd put the top down so we could enjoy the moonlight. So I went to work and got the top down in about an hour and...

Bill: (Interrupting) An hour! I got mine down in two minutes.

Fred: Sure, but you have a convertible.

Mail Order

Characters: Storekeeper, Farmer

Scene: A hardware store

(As the scene opens, the farmer is just entering the store.)

Storekeeper: Good morning, sir. How can I help you?

Farmer: I'm looking for an axe.

Storekeeper: (Shows him two or three, in pantomime). This is a very fine one.

Farmer: (He examines them and decides on one.) How much is this one?

Storekeeper: It is $1.50.

Farmer: (Produces a page torn from a mail order catalogue.) Look here, this is that very axe for only $1.33.

Storekeeper: (after looking at the picture and pondering) I suppose if they can sell it for that, so can I.

Farmer: Okay, I'll take it.

Storekeeper: (Picking up the axe, he puts it on the scales and weighs it; he then makes out a bill for $1.33 plus 15 cents (figuring aloud).

Farmer: (Shouting) Hey! What's that 15 cents for?

Storekeeper: For postage. If you sent for it, you'd have to pay postage, wouldn't you?

Farmer: Well, ah...I guess I would. (He counts aloud.) $1.48.

Storekeeper: (Wraps the axe and calmly lays it on the shelf behind him.)

Farmer: Say! What's the big idea?

Storekeeper: Come back in three days, and you can have it.

Lifeline

Characters: Harry, a patient in the hospital; Jim, his friend

Scene: Hospital room

(As the scene opens, Jim is standing by the bed of Harry.)

Jim: I'm sure sorry to see you looking so bad.

Harry: (Gasping for breath) Don't grieve so, friend. I want you to know that I'm leaving you my money, my cars, my plane, my country estate, my yacht — everything!

Jim: Thank you, thank you. You're much too good to me. If there was only something I could do for you!

Harry: (Nods head, gasping. He can't get out any words.)

Jim: Do you want to tell me something else?

Harry: (Again nods head. Gasping even more.)

Jim: You don't have the strength to tell me. Can you write it? (He runs and gets a pad and a pencil and gives it to Harry.)

(Harry feebly writes a few words and then falls back unconscious.)

Jim: I wonder if he's leaving me his townhouse. (He reads the message.) "You are standing on my air hose."

The Elevator Operator

Characters: Sam, Bill, Elevator Operator

Scene: Inside an elevator

(Bill and Sam are riding in an elevator to their office.)

Sam: Boy, do I get tired waiting for elevators.

Bill: Yes, but think how tired you'd be if you had to walk up ten flights to your office.

Sam: Well, sometimes I feel like I'd rather walk than wait, especially when the operator turns out to be one of those smart alecks.

Bill: What do you mean?

Sam: You never can tell what an elevator operator is going to do. He will give you a lift one minute and run you down the next and always gives you evasive or misleading answers.

Bill: Don't blame him. Why everybody knows an elevator man has his ups and downs.

Sam: Even if he does, he can be civil, can't he?

Bill: Just don't judge him to harshly.

Operator: (who has been taking all this in) Tenth floor, out please.

Bill: (Aside) I'll just show my friend how wrong he is about this fellow.

Bill: (To the operator) Tell me, my good man, if the cable should break on this elevator, would we go up or down?

Operator: (Tired of the same old questions) Mister, it all depends on the kind of life you've led.

Miss America

A volunteer from the audience is picked (best if well known). He then is directed to walk on an imaginary line on the floor as straight and as well as possible. The volunteer repeats this again going the opposite way, except that he puts one hand on his hip and extends the other in the air. Finally, the audience sings, here she comes, Miss America."

The Human Car

Four people get on their hands and knees and are assigned to be the four wheels of an automobile. Another is placed down in front of the car and acts as a starter. (Crank the hair.) Then there is a couple who are going on a date. There are various options, such as a flat tire and engine trouble. Use your imagination for more ideas.

The German Soldier

The German commanding officer is walking with his three men, who are marching single file. The soldier at the end sneezes, and the officer turns around to the soldier right behind him and asks him if he sneezed. The soldier denies it, and the officer shoots the soldier. Repeat again. Finally, the actual sneezer is the only one left, and he sneezes for the third and last time, and the officer halts, turns around, and asks the soldier if he sneezed. The soldier says, "Yes," and the German officer says, "Gesundheit."

The Reporter

The reporter is on the edge of an imaginary cliff and says to himself, "Life isn't worth living, for I haven't made up one newsworthy story yet." A passerby stops the reporter just in time, and they talk about the situation. The visitor tells the reporter of his problems, and then they both decide to jump together. A final passerby stops them just before they jump, and the same thing happens, so they all agree to jump. They all chant "1, 2, 3, JUMP!" All but the reporter jump, and he says to himself, "What a real story this will make!"

The Monster:

A "monster" is led in by another "guy" with a leash around the monster's neck and a covering over his head.

The "guy" tells the audience that this is the ugliest monster in the world, and he calls for three "prepared" female volunteers from the audience. The first one comes up and looks under the covering and screams; the next one faints, and the last one barfs. In conclusion, a highly respected, well-known volunteer is asked to look, and the monster looks back at the volunteer, throws a tantrum, and dies.

The Two Monsters

In the middle of any sort of meeting or gathering, two ferocious monsters run into the room and chase each other without ever touching, and eventually the two run out. A little later, the two monsters reappear and act the same as before except, right at the end, one of the two monsters touches the other and says, "Tag. You're *it!*"

The Fixer

by Minnie L. Peterson

Time: Five minutes

Characters: Bill, the suitor; Phil, his friend; Lil, beloved of Bill; Mr. Pill, Lil's father

Scene I

The scene opens with Lil seated in an attentive attitude and Bill nervously pacing the floor. Bill finally works up the necessary courage and proposes (using suitable local form)

Lil: Oh, Bill, this is so sudden! You must talk to father. You know how he is; he wants me to marry well, but when he knows you, I'm sure he won't object.

Bill: Aw, Lil, I hate to do that. The old gentleman might kick me out. Let's elope!

Lil: No, we can't do that. You must talk to Father, but I'll tell you what you can do. If you haven't the nerve to face him alone, bring along a friend who can put in a good word for you occasionally and so help matters along.

Bill: That's a good idea. I'll bring Phil over tonight, and by the time we get through talking with your father, he'll be tickled to death to let me marry you. S'long.

Scene II

Bill: Now listen, Phil, all you have to do is sit still, take in all I say, and just make it a little bigger and better. For instance, if I say I own a Ford, you must laugh and say, "Ford nothing — why, he owns a Cadillac." Get the idea? Pretend I have an inferiority complex. That will make a hit with the old gent.

Phil: Sure, I getcha! You say something, and I just play it up big.

Bill: Shh! Here he comes. Oh! Good evening, Mr. Pill. How are you?

Pa: So-so. Sit down. What's this I hear about you wanting to marry my daughter? Have you any money?

Bill: Yes, I have a bank account.

Phil: Bank account — listen to that! Ha, ha! Why, Mr. Pill, he's president of a bank!

Pa: Hmm! Is that so? Well then, tell me, have you got a home you can move into when you get married?

Bill: Why, yes, I have a modest little six-room bungalow.

Phil: Man, how he raves! Why, Mr. Pill, he has a twenty-room house with six bathrooms, an indoor swimming pool, built-in pianos, and wall plugs for his Vitaphone.

Pa: Well, for a young man you have done remarkably well. And no doubt you own a car?

Bill: Yes, a little Chevrolet.

Phil: Can you beat that? Why, Mr. Pill, his Rolls-Royce is the talk of the neighborhood — custom-built body, fourteen cylinders.

(Bill kicks his leg to make him stop, then starts to cough.)

Pa: Oh, you have a cough, haven't you? Too bad!

Bill: Well, yes, a slight cough.

Phil: (Excitedly.) A slight cough — a slight cough! Listen to the man! Why Mr. Pill, that's consumption, real consumption, and he's got it in both lungs!

(The father kicks Bill and Phil out and stamps off angrily.)

The End

Greek Tragedy

Chorus: (Claps slow, slow, quick, quick, slow throughout the stunt. Characters speak to this rhythm and repeat each line several times. Chorus enters while repeating, "We are members of the chorus.")

Father: (Enters) "I am the father of the story. My daughter must marry the villain for his filthy money." (Off)

Daughter: (Enters) I am the daughter of the story. (Repeat)

Father: You must marry the villain for his filthy money. (Exits)

Daughter: Oh, oh! What shall I do? Oh, oh! What shall I do?

Hero: I am the hero of the story. I have come to save you. I have come to save you.

Daughter: I must marry the villain, for my father has decreed it. I cannot bear to live. (Kills self — drinks poison)

Hero: I cannot bear to live. (Repeats action of daughter)

Mother: I am the mother of the story. Oh, oh! What has happened? Oh, oh! I cannot stand it! (Stabs self) Ug, ug, ug, ug, ug.

Villain: I have come to claim the beauty. Oh, oh! Who has done this? Oh, oh! I cannot bear it. (Cuts throat — draws hand across throat in rhythm and makes appropriate sound)

Father: I am to blame for this. Oh, oh! What can I do? (Stabs self in stomach, makes sound as he dies)

Chorus: This is the end of the story. (Exit)

(Audience *hiss* villain and *cheer* hero.)

The Brutal Miner

Give the following characters and sounds each to a group of people; then read or tell the story. As each character is mentioned, the proper group rises, makes the appropriate noise, and sits down.

Characters

Brutal Miner	"Grr"
Tired Wife	"Oh, dear!"
A Lazy Son	"(Yawns) Oh-h"
Young Daughter	"Tee Hee"
Beautiful Daughter	"Ah"
Handsome Harry	"Ah ha"
Auto	"Honk Honk"
Cat	"Meow"

Once upon a time in the far west, there lived a brutal miner ("Grr"), who had a tired wife ("Oh, dear!"), a lazy son ("[Yawns] Oh-h"), a giggling young daughter ("Tee Hee"), and a beautiful daughter ("Ah"). On the other side of the mountain lived Handsome Harry ("Ah ha"). This young man drove his auto ("Honk Honk") over the mountains and carried the mail to the brutal miner ("Grr").

One day the tired wife ("Oh, dear!") was cleaning the house, and the beautiful daughter ("Ah") was helping her. The young daughter ("Tee Hee") was playing with the cat ("Meow") on the steps. The brutal miner ("Grr"), came out and kicked the cat ("Meow"). The tired wife ("Oh, dear!") and the beautiful daughter ("Ah") rushed out with brooms and hit the brutal miner ("Grr") but this did not bother him. He grabbed the tired mother ("Oh, dear!") by one arm and the beautiful daughter ("Ah") by the other and shoved them into the house. The young daughter ("Tee Hee") ran away with the cat ("Meow").

Just then Handsome Harry ("Ah ha") drove up in his auto ("Honk Honk") and saw the brutal miner ("Grr") abusing the tired wife ("Oh, dear!") and the beautiful daughter ("Ah"). Handsome Harry ("Ah ha") rushed to the rescue and grabbed the brutal miner ("Grr") and threw him down the mine shaft. The beautiful daughter ("Ah") flew into the waiting arms of Handsome Harry ("Ah ha"), while the tired wife ("Oh, dear!") and the young daughter ("Tee Hee") watched with enthusiasm.

Handsome Harry ("Ah ha") took the beautiful daughter ("Ah") in his auto ("Honk Honk") to the little church in the wild woods, and they lived happily ever after.

Thus ends the story of the brutal miner ("Grr") who met his fate at the hands of Handsome Harry ("Ah ha"), who married the beautiful daughter ("Ah"). The brutal miner's ("Grr") insurance cared nicely for the tired wife ("Oh, dear!"), the lazy son ("[Yawns] Oh-h"), the young daughter ("Tee Hee"), and the cat ("Meow").

Little Baby Foo-Foo

Characters: Narrator, Rabbit (Little Baby Foo-Foo), Field Mouse, Fairy Godmother

Sing: Little Baby Foo-Foo running through the forest catching all the field mice and bashing them on the head.

Narrator: Along comes the fairy godmother and she says...

Fairy Godmother: Little Baby Foo-Foo, that's not very nice to hit the poor little field mice on the head. I don't ever want to see it happen again!

Narrator: But the very next day...

(Repeat from the beginning two more times.)

Fairy Godmother: (Third time) Little Baby Foo-Foo, I've warned you and warned you not to hit the mice, so now I'm going to turn you into a goon!

Narrator: And she did! The moral of the story is "Hare today, goon tomorrow."

The Viper

Setting: The palace of a beautiful queen and handsome king

ME — Time: When days pass as if they were seconds, B.C. February 1957.

ME: The king and queen are having a discussion when suddenly a servant rushes up to the monarchs and bows.

1st Servant: Your majesties, your majesties, a viper is coming in 500 years!

Queen: Thank you servant. If that is all, you may be dismissed.

(Servant leaves.)

ME: The king and queen are reading books and a servant rushes up to them and bows low.

2nd Servant: King, Queen, the viper is coming in 100 years.

(The queen now turns to the King.)

Queen: King, you must do something about it.

King: Yes, dear. Servant — warn the guards.

Queen: Thank you King.

ME: Now the king and queen are meditating with their eyes closed. Suddenly another servant comes running up to the throne, bows, and says loudly:

3rd Servant: Your highnesses, your highnesses! The viper is coming in 50 years! 50 years!

King: (The king wakes up with a start and yells) "Send the guards to the gates! Organize the servants! Warn all the subjects! Don't just stand there — GO!

(The servant runs out.)

ME: Now one of the servants runs in and whispers something in the king's ear.

King: (The king stands up and says) Show the viper in.

(The viper enters and goes up to the king.)

Viper: I am de Viper. I vish to vash and vipe de vindows.

ME: Everyone is so overjoyed with relief. They all bow three times to the viper and praise him.

A Case in Court

Bailiff: (Enters) Everybody stand.

(Judge enters, carrying an old bench.)

Bailiff: This court is now in session, and the judge is on his bench.

Judge: (Judge raps for order with his gavel.) Please be seated.

Bailiff: Case number one.

Judge: Did you know _____ was in court last week?

Bailiff: Is that so? In what suit?

Judge: Oh, just his old suit.

Bailiff: No, no. What was he charged with?

Judge: Well the way he was acting, I think he was charged with soda water.

Bailiff: Case number two.

Neighbor versus _____.

Judge: Mr. Bailiff, bring in _____. _____, we have a complaint here signed by some of your neighbors. Last week a cat got caught in a tree, and when your neighbors asked you to rescue the cat, you refused, saying you were afraid to climb the tree for fear you would run into a naked limb. Case dismissed.

Bailiff: Case number three.

Case of Mrs. _____ versus the neighbors.

Judge: Bailiff, bring Mrs. _____ to the stand. Mrs. _____ will plead her own case. I think she is competent. A woman of many words. Mrs. _____, your neighbors have charged you with illuminated negligence. They claim when they were passing your home last night that your blinds were not drawn, and they stood and watched you undress and jump into bed with your husband.

Mrs.: My husband wasn't home last night, Judge. The joke's on you.

Bailiff: Case number four.

(Man and woman enter, sit down.)

Judge: According to the complaint, I see these people want a divorce. The complaint further alleges that these parties are dumb but not deaf. Glad they aren't absentminded. (To man and woman) So you want a divorce. (To woman) What is your husband's name?

Woman: (Play *Kelly with Green Necktie)*

Judge: I see. Your husband's name is Kelly. (To man) And your wife's name, please?

Man: (Stands and plays *Sweet Alice Ben Bolt)*

Judge: Yes, I remember Alice. How long have you known each other?

Both: (Play *School Days)*

Judge: So you have known each other since school days. Do you remember where you were when you proposed to her?

Both: (Play *Down by the Old Mill Stream)*

Judge: Down by the old mill stream. How romantic. Do you remember how you were dressed or looked on that occasion? (Judge asks for water.)

Both: (Play *When You Wore a Tulip)*

Judge: What time of year were you married?

Both: (Play *Springtime in the Rockies)*

Judge: How many children have you?

Both: (Play *John Brown had a Little Indian)*

(Woman raises a finger for each boy.)

Judge: Ten sons. What a wonderful family. Yet you want a divorce from this man. (Woman nods.) What are your grounds for divorce?

Woman: (Play *Won't Come Home until Morning)*

Judge: So he won't come home until morning? So that's it. (To man.) And where are you all night?

Man: (Play *Hail, Hail, the Gangs Are Here)*

Judge: Oh, I see, he's out carousing with the gang—good ol' days. I see myself now, how thirsty. (To woman) And what were you doing while he was out all night?

Woman: (Play *Rock-a-bye Baby)*

Judge: (To man) I can't understand how a man with a farm and ten fine sons can do as you have done. Think what a wonderful time you could have in your home.

(Man looks ashamed.)

Judge: (To man) Do you want another chance to make your home what it could be? Do you want to try again?

Man: (Kneels to woman and plays *Let Me Call You Sweetheart)*

Judge: (To woman) You really love this man, don't you?

Woman: (Plays *I Love You Truly)*

Judge: Good luck to you both. Better luck this time. Court adjourned.

Really Getting Together

I suppose all of us have our own favorite reason for having family reunions. In a way they are extensions of family home evenings. Family reunions are an opportunity to gather our larger, eternal families together to learn to understand and love one another; and to unite ourselves in the work of the Lord, just as we do in family home evenings.

Having positive, enjoyable experiences together cements family relationships. Having fun together is a powerful and effective way to draw a family together. The lasting memories that are formed in well-planned family reunions will add to the respect and love that we hope to have for each other throughout eternity.

In addition, family reunions provide an opportunity for the younger family members to become acquainted with their relatives and their heritage. Perhaps this heritage is part of the sealing force between the children and the fathers to which Elijah referred. Through this heritage everyone has a chance to tie himself to a family in a patriarchal order.

Reunions are an excellent way to organize and gather genealogical information and to stimulate genealogical research. Often we spend a great deal of time researching our ancestors, while failing to record the marriages, new babies, temple endowments, and other information of our own family.

An essential step to successful reunions is organizing the family. A family organization is not complete until a chairman has been chosen to direct and supervise reunions for the family. The chairman may keep this position for many years. His responsibilities should include determining where and when the family would like the reunion and suggesting an enthusiastic relative from the chosen locality to be the director of the reunion. This director should be appointed yearly, but approved by all at the reunion. He might be responsible for choosing a vice-chairman, a secretary, and a treasurer. We have found that it is helpful for the secretary and the treasurer to live in the same locality as the director.

Selecting the wrong time of year for a family get-together can be disastrous. The best time is when the most members of the family can attend, perhaps when the family is already free for a state or national holiday. A helpful idea is to schedule the reunion for the same time each year.

The selection of a place for a family reunion will also be a key factor in its success. If the theme of the reunion calls for a lot of genealogical papers to be spread out and a lot of writing to be done by many people, it should be indoors, under shelter from wind and rain. If there is a large banquet involving a lot of food and babies, a ward or stake cultural hall might be considered. For summertime reunions, look for a good grassy spot where the youth can play. A fenced-in area with plenty of play equipment will require fewer adults to supervise the toddlers. Families that enjoy volleyball, softball, and footraces should find a location with plenty of space. Trees are useful not only for shade but also for all types of swings and recreational equipment. When a temple session is on the program, the reunion should be near a temple.

Reunion activities should be planned around a theme, which should also be evident in the invitation and the program. For example, a reunion with the theme of "heritage" could include favorite songs of Great-Grandfather and century-old dances. For decorations, old farm machinery, scrubbing boards, and other old tools could be used. The activity section of the program might include games and activities that great-grandfather played. Old-timers could participate in the program by telling what it was like when they were young. There could also be a skit about a humorous event in

the life of one of the ancestors. The important factor in selecting a theme is to find a concept that will give unity to the various activities of the reunion.

Making creative, original, and unique invitations may take a little thinking, but they can make a great contribution to the success of the reunion. Often a family will decide to attend simply on the strength of a creative invitation. Besides announcing the theme, time, and place, an invitation could mention the program and the fun things that are going to happen and ask for a response indicating who will attend. The reunion director should send announcements to everyone concerned, from newlyweds to older folks. A picture of last year's reunion, the up-to-date history of the family, and a newsletter could all be included. The invitation could also invite each family to come prepared to take part on the program or remind everyone to bring genealogical information.

The director of the reunion should be aware of the equipment needed: a source of electrical power, lights, cameras, screens, microphone, loud speakers, overhead projectors, film projectors, slide projectors, a record player, a tape recorder, etc. All genealogical equipment, including blank family group sheets, pedigree charts, old family pictures, family histories, and other genealogy forms could also be provided. Tables are needed for eating, doing genealogy, and making displays of books of remembrance and old family pictures. Name tags, a first aid kit, and extra games are often useful also.

When the reunion finally takes place, remember that everyone wants to be where the action is and to feel comfortable and relaxed. At a canyon reunion, activities could include several kinds of ball games — softball, volleyball, etc. These types of games not only interest a lot of people, but can easily absorb new people as they arrive.

Shyness will not last long if the activity director for the reunion has planned for the young as well as the older folks. Swings, frisbees, and other simple game equipment interest the young. A cable with a pulley swing tied between two trees will make an exciting swing.

If the reunion is held indoors, useful items are name tags

and a large paper tree on the wall that each person can sign; it's fun for family members to find which branch they belong to and write their names on it. Some fabric games or indoor games can be played by any number of people; best are those that can absorb new players at any time. By minor changes in equipment, outdoor games such as softball, volleyball, or hockey can he modified so they can be played indoors.

After everyone has arrived and become tired of free-play activities, the activity director should lead a game that will help the group gather into one area. Relay races, sawdust scrambles, and competitive games are usually the most enjoyable at this point. Several adults may be needed to arrange starting lines into age groups; others are needed to be judges and to hand out prizes (see page 36).

When the clan is fired of physical activities, it's time to rest. This is a good opportunity for the program. A good program gives everyone a chance to get acquainted, and can be as much fun as any part of the reunion. Be careful, though, that the program isn't the same year after year.

An exciting part of the program may be when grandpa and grandma tell stories of their younger days and sing the songs that were popular when they fell in love. It will be a spiritual feast to hear the report of a newly returned missionary. Some families select a different ancestor to honor each year. Even though some families may not come prepared to participate on the program, the MC could bring some readings or skits that can be done impromptu by those families.

If the MC plans to arrange the various numbers in any sequence, he may want to visit the families before the program begins and find out what each number is. Programs never drag with a prepared and enthusiastic MC.

Just before or just after the program are times to eat, if a meal is part of the agenda. Some families have established a tradition of barbecuing a whole leg of beef for large reunions. Other families eat the same fare that great-grandmother once prepared.

One of the last items on the agenda may be the organizational meeting in which you plan the next reunion. The chairman takes charge long enough to select a new reunion director, time, and place. The new reunion director may want a few minutes to discuss ideas for the next reunion and to select new officers to help him. An up-to-date list of addresses and any reunion records should be turned over to the new officers. If the youth have a voice in what projects are planned, they will support them more fully.

Family home evenings are one of the most important meetings conducted among Church members today. Family reunions, could be just as important. In one sense, when the family prepares and holds family reunions they are also preparing for eternity.

A good way to learn to love our relatives is to spend time together in well-planned family reunions. A family reunion can be a very personal and privileged gathering. If you have never organized your family for a reunion, start now — you will receive joy far beyond your expectations. Yes, there will be discouragements. Some family members will say they don't have time or that they are too busy. But the rewards more than compensate for the discouragements.

It was our Father in Heaven who first gathered us together in a great family reunion. Certainly we must have discussed our future, our leaders, and many other aspects of our lives ahead. If our future families are to be together for eternity, why not start now to establish firm, loving, and powerful relationships in our own patriarchal orders through family reunions?

Family Reunions are Making a Comeback

By Marilyn Hoffman
the Christian Science Monitor

NEW YORK — The people are rediscovering their families, and family reunions are enjoying a comeback. Folks these days are making the effort, setting aside the time, traveling the distances, providing the point that although family members may be out of sight, they are most certainly not out of memory.

Reunions pin down good intentions about visiting far-flung relatives and help to meet the challenge of maintaining or refreshing long-distance relationships.

Clan gatherings have been encouraged by Better Homes and Gardens for three years now as a means of encouraging family unity and keeping the reunion tradition alive.

In 1986 the magazine even persuaded President Reagan to sign a proclamation, declaring the first weekend in August (Aug. 5 to 7 this year) as "National Family Reunion Weekend."

The President's sentiments included these words: "Family reunions bridge generations and remind us of our roots. I encourage all families to use the family reunion to lap these roots again and to renew their pledge of love and concern for each other."

In a Better Homes and Gardens Family Network survey, more than 70 percent of respondents said they had attended at least one reunion and, on average, reported having gone to nearly four. The survey also revealed that one-third of respondents do hold or plan to hold reunions on a regular basis.

Seventy percent said at family members had become increasingly important to them over the last five years and that they wished they could spend more time with them. Most said they look to the idea of a family reunion because they want to be together and to "rekindle ties and new relatives." Many indicated they wanted to learn more about their family heritage and see photographs and hear stories of their ancestors.

An average of 39 family members attended the last reunion attended by those surveyed. One-third of the events were held outdoors in a park or garden (and more than a quarter were held outdoors in a park or garden) and more than a quarter were held in residences. About a tenth were in halls, restaurants, country clubs, or hotels.

Although nearly three-quarters of those responding said they enjoyed themselves very much at reunions, about three percent said they didn't enjoy themselves much.

Brooks Rogers, a New York career woman, along with a brother and a sister, went down South last year to attend their first family reunion. They had all read the family history that had been put together in a booklet by a self-appointed family historian and were curious to meet the people, many of whom were strangers to them.

Class Reunion 1932-1984

A Different World, But in Many Ways the Best of Times

High School graduation reunion can be a competitive sport. At early reunions, classmates compete with each other about jobs and incomes; at the 25th, it's spouses and children. After that, they brag about their grandchildren and vacation homes while regarding, with envy or glee, classmates waistlines, hairlines, and wrinklelines.

With a 45th reunion comes a new phase of competition, the one described by Woody Allen when he said, "Ninety percent of life is just showing up." It is said there are Three Ages of Women: youth, middle-age, and "you haven't changed."

But change is the name of the game. Consider. Graduates of the class of '32 were before the pill and the population explosion which inexplicably went hand in hand so to speak.

We were before NuSkin, WordPerfect, television, penicillin, polio shots, antibiotics, and Frisbees. Before frozen food, nylon, dacron, Xerox, Kinsey. We were before radar, fluorescent lights, credit cards and ball-point pens. For us, time-sharing meant togetherness, not computers; a chip meant a piece of wood; hardware meant hardware, and software wasn't even a word. Before air travel went commercial, almost no one flew across the country, and transatlantic flights belonged to Lindbergh and Amelia Earhart. Before Israel and the United Nations. Before India, Pakistan, Indonesia, the Philippines, and Iceland were independent countries. Since our graduation, 92 countries — 48 of them African — have become independent nations. And, God help us all, we were before the cataclysm of nuclear fission.

We were before pantihose and drip-dry clothes. Before ice makers, dishwashers, clothes dryers, freezers, and electric blankets. Before Alaska and Hawaii became states. Before men wore long hair and earrings, and women wore tuxedos.

We were before Leonard Bernstein, yogurt, Ann Landers, plastics, hair dryers, the 40-hour work week, and the minimum wage. We got married first and then lived together. How quaint can you be?

In our time, closets were for clothes, not coming out of, and a book about two young women living together in Europe could be called "Our Hearts were Young and Gay." We were before Grandma Moses and Frank Sinatra and cup-sizing for bras. We wore Peter Pan collars and thought a deep cleavage was something butchers did.

We were before Batman, Grapes of Wrath, Rudolph, the Red-nosed Reindeer, Snoopy, DDT and vitamin pills, disposable diapers, Jeeps, the Jefferson Memorial and the Jefferson nickel. When we were in school, pizzas, Cheerios, frozen orange juice, instant coffee, and McDonalds were unheard of. We though fast food was what you ate during Lent.

We were before Citizen Kane, J.D. Salinger, and Chiquita Banana. Before FM radio, tape recorders, electric typewriters, word processors, IBM, electronic music, disco dancing, and no such coined word as teenager. Then we were just parents and children, older or younger.

In our day cigarette smoking was fashionable, grass was mowed, coke was something you drank, and pot was something you cooked in or kept under the bed. We were before day-care centers, house-husbands, baby-sitters, computer dating, dual careers, and commuter marriages. In 1932 American schools were not desegregated, "made in Japan" meant junk, and the term "making out" referred to how you did on an exam.

In our time there were 5 and 10 cent stores where you could buy things for 5 and 10 cents. For just one nickel you could ride the street car or make a phone call or buy a pop or get two copies of the Salt Lake Tribune — and receive change, or buy enough stamps to mail one letter and two postcards. You could buy a new Chevy Coupe for $659, but who could afford it in 1932? Nobody. A pity, too, because gas was 11 cents a gallon.

If anyone in those days had asked us to explain CIA, UFO, IBM, NATO, Ms., NFL, SATs, JFK, ERA, or IUD, we would have said alphabet soup. We were not before the difference in the sexes was discovered, but we were before sex change. We just made do with what we had. And we were the last generation that was so dumb as to think you needed a husband to have a baby! No Wash 'N Wear clothes for us, and if we had sheets, pillow slips, tablecloths, or napkins, they had to be ironed.

We had girdles with garters on them, bloomers for gym and petticoats, and 10 o'clock curfews. In those days we had humorists that were funny — Benchley, Charlie Chaplin, W.C. — Fields, Laurel and Hardy, Hackenbush taking a pulse and saying, "Either this man is dead or my watch has stopped."

We had fountain pens and bottles of real ink. Our stockings were made of real silk with seams in the back that were never straight. We danced in big halls to the big band music like Tommy Dorsey, Glenn Gray, Guy Lombardo, and Benny Goodman. Unlike the remote-control dancers of today, we knew how it felt to have your partner hold you close and double dip. We played thick 78 RPM records with cactus needles that always needed sharpening, were saddle oxfords, and had cars with rumble seats. And when Ray Noble played "The Very Thought of You" on his piano or Bing Crosby crooned "When the Blue of the Night Meets the Gold of the Day," we melted.

In the springtime of my senility, I am a misfit. I don't go in for consciousness raising or sensitivity training, jogging or aerobics. I can't pump my own gas, nor do I want to learn how. My legs are white and my stockings are suntan even when the opposite is in style. I'm not "into" veggies or Yoga or Zen or Punk. The man I live with is my husband, and after 45 years he's still the same one.

Remember the black sateen bloomers and the long black stockings we wore in grade school? The "tight" pants of our day were baggy compared to the blue jeans of today. We were L-O-N-G before the "itsy bitsy teeny weeny yellow polka dot bikini!"

Kith and Kin...

If you could see your ancestors
Standing in a row,
Would you be proud of them or not,
Or don't you really know?
Some strange discoveries are made
In climbing family trees,
And some of them you know
Do not particularly please.
If you could see your ancestors
All standing in a row,
There might be some of them, perhaps,
You wouldn't care to know.
But here's another question, which
Requires a different view.
If you could see your ancestors
Would they be proud of you?

—Anon

Genealogy Songs (Medley of Commercials)

Words and Arrangements by Jane Thompson, BYU Program Bureau

Chevrolet Song

The Psychology of genealogy
Is when you trace your family line.
You are bound to see that your pedigree
To you will be a document divine.
When you keep on writing, and it gets exciting
When one turns out to be your great-grandmother
So come along with me, do genealogy.
Get busy on your fam'ly line…And

Colgate Song

Fill your family group sheets.
Do a little every day
And get it done… (What a FEELING)
You will shout and say…

Winston Song

My line looks good, like a (clap, clap) pedigree should.
You'll soon be way back to (clap, clap) Adam, who'll say
the secret ingredient in genealogy is…people.

Chock-Full-O-Nuts Song

Chock-full-of-folks is your heavenly fam'ly,
heavenly fam'ly,
heavenly fam'ly.
Chock-full-of-folks is your heavenly fam'ly
With an eternity of happiness that money can't buy.

Chevrolet Song

So... Come a...long with me.
Do genealogy.
Get busy on your fam'ly line...
Umwah. (That means throw a kiss like Dinah Shore.)

Books Written by Alma and Marie Heaton

Price list for activity books/video, cassette tapes, and records.

If you are raising a family, teaching class, or directing an activity, these books are a must! The purpose of earth life is to gain experience. Serve that purpose! If questions, call Alma Heaton (Telephone — 801-375-9541, address — 235 South 900 East, Provo, Utah 84606.)

Prices subject to change without notice. Add mailing and handling costs.

After Retirement Enjoy yourself it's later than you think. $9.95

Attention Getters and Forfeits Includes ideas to act get group's attention, forfeits and consequences. $7.95

Behind the Taj Mahal Experiences of Alma and Marie's International Mission in India for 18 months — exciting, amazing, thrilling, disappointing, antagonizing, aggravating, heartbreaking, spiritual, uplifting, and testimony building. $15.95

Big Talk from Babes Pictures and captions of babies in a dance class. $14.95

The Book of Alma A joint oral history project, Brigham Young University Archives. Alma Heaton was interviewed by David Whittaker. $12.95

Dance Books (1) *Social Dance Rhythms*, $6.95 (2) *American Dance Rhythms*, $4.95 (3) *Fun Dance Rhythms*, $21.95 (4) *Advanced Dance Rhythms*, $3.95 (5) *Techniques of Teaching Dance*, $17.95 (6) *Close Dancing with Donny & Marie*, $4.95 (7) *Disco Line Dancing with Donny & Marie*, $4.95 (8) *Ballroom and Social Dance Rhythms*, $9.95 (9) *Latin Dances, Beginners*, $5.95 (10) *Latin Dances Advanced*, $5.95

Did You Think to Pray? Students in trouble. $7.95

Directing Activities Contains plans and ideas for all kinds of activities and parties; helpful for MC. $9.95

Double Fun Ideas and tips on how to make games for outdoor and indoor activities. These games have been shown on TV., Real People, PM Magazine, KBYU, and Bonneville International. $7.95

Enjoy Yourself — It's Later Than You Think This book helps people at all ages. $8.95

Experiences of Jonathon Heaton and His Fifteen Sons $9.95

Experiences of Isreal Heaton and His Four Sons $14.95

Experiences of Delaun Heaton $14.95

Experiences of Alma Heaton Life History. $21.95

Experience of a Lifetime Experiences that taught BYU students the greatest lessons. $9.95

Family Do Book Includes all types of family activities, outings, family home evenings, etc. $7.95

Family Recreation Activities that develop family unity, harmony, and togetherness. $7.95

Finding Gold in Your Golden Years Grow older without growing old. $9.95

G-Rated Jokes and Other Rarities Outlines useful ideas and jokes for the master of ceremonies at parties. $7.95

G-Rated Jokes #2 Jokes for many purposes. $7.95

Games Our Pioneers Played $10.95

Games with Gospel Themes Games that are designed to be appropriate for the Sabbath day. $8.95

Get Acquainted with Ice Breakers Includes paper and pencil games for parties. $8.95

Gospel Criss-Cross Mazes Criss-cross mazes are blocks of letters in which words relating to gospel themes are concealed horizontally, vertically, or diagonally. Keeps children busy while traveling. $8.95

Gospel Crossword Puzzles Includes crossword puzzles on many gospel topics: Temple work, Book of Mormon, Old Testament, Word of Wisdom, Presidents of the Church, etc. Excellent for traveling games. Quiets class members as they enter the classroom. $11.95

Gospel Learning Motivators Includes challenging quizzes, paper and pencil games. Games for all age groups. Book is designed so that the pages may be easily duplicated. Good openers for classes. $7.95

Helps for Parents and Teachers Teaching games on many subjects for family home evening, church classes, also a reference book. $10.95

The Joy of Living Your Religion This book tells you "who" is living their religion. $11.95

The LDS Games Book Games for parties, family home evenings, firesides, etc. Games are appropriate for home evenings, firesides, and Sunday lessons. Lesson applications are in the back of the book. $14.95

Live & Learn These experiences contain thoughts that will improve your talks and give you ideas of how to write your family history. Gives ideas and help for translating your experiences into valuable lessons. Applications to life are written after each experience. $10.95

Mormon Book of Fun Contains activities for ward, stake, class, and group parties. $7.95

One Liners Why use two lines when one will do? Notes from talks over the years. $10.95

Party Starters and Quiet Games Includes ice breakers and get-acquainted games for all types of parties. $6.95

Playway of Teaching Games for 30 BYU academic subjects and trivia questions. $14.95

Professor of Fun A dissertation presented to the Department of Physical Education, Brigham Young University. In partial fulfillment for the requirements of the degree of Doctor of Education. $17.95

Recreation in the LDS Family Words only give meaning after the student has had the experience. Includes *Playway of Learning*, using games, objects, visual aids and experiences. $22.95

Reunions: How and What to Do at Family Reunions:$7.95

Teaching with Objects Object lessons for gospel topics. $9.95

Tools for Teaching This book contains a variety of learning experiences. The tools quickly focus the students' attention on the subject matter. $9.95

Traveling Games Keeps people happy and busy on long trips. $8.95

Visual Lessons: These visual aids have a lesson written on the back of the pictures. Keeps students attention on the subject while you give the lesson. $17.95

Worshiping the Wrong Hero $10.95

Video Tapes Showing students demonstrating the activities written in the books: dances, games, ragballs made from worn-out socks, bowling balls, frisbees, innertubes, crutches, stilts. $50.00